THE NATURAL DYE HANDBOOK

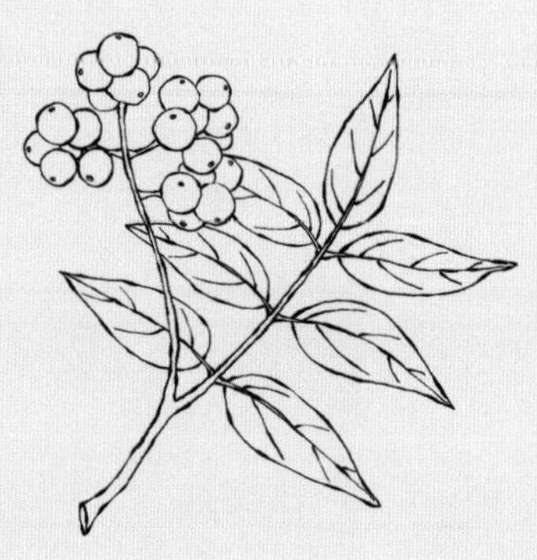

THE NATURAL DYE HANDBOOK

A comprehensive guide to exploring plant-based dyeing techniques

HEIDI IVERSON

DAVID & CHARLES
—PUBLISHING—

www.davidandcharles.com

A DAVID AND CHARLES BOOK

David and Charles is an imprint of David and Charles, Ltd
Suite A, Tourism House, Pynes Hill, Exeter, EX2 5WS

Conceived, edited, and designed by Quarto Publishing, an imprint of
The Quarto Group, 1 Triptych Place, London, SE1 9SH

First published in the UK and USA in 2025

A catalogue record for this book is available from the British Library.

ISBN-13: 9781446314760 Hardback
ISBN-13: 9781446314784 EPUB

This book has been printed on paper from approved suppliers and made from pulp from sustainable sources.

Printed in China.

10 9 8 7 6 5 4 3 2 1

Assistant editor: Ella Whiting
Copy editor: Philippa Wilkinson
Designer: Joanna Bettles
Photography: Dave Burton and Jess Esposito (cover and swatches),
Whitni Rader (lifestyle photography)
Art director: Martina Calvio
Managing editor: Emma Harverson
Publisher: Lorraine Dickey
Production manager: David Hearn

Extra interior images: Insung Yoon/Unsplash (page 11); Evannovostro/Shutterstock (page 15); S Zaggi/Shutterstock (page 20).

David and Charles publishes high-quality books on a wide range of subjects. For more information visit www.davidandcharles.com.

Follow us on Instagram by searching for @dandcbooks.

Layout of the digital edition of this book may vary depending on reader hardware and display settings.

Contents

Meet Heidi

Hi friends, my name is Heidi. I'm originally from the Midwest, where I grew up on a farm near a small town in Northwest Iowa. I studied ceramics, sculpture, and printmaking at the University of South Dakota before moving to Northern California 20 years ago. I now live on the ancestral lands of the Native American Coast Miwok and Southern Pomo tribes in West Sonoma County in Northern California. I'm a textile artist, teacher, natural dye advocate, and founding member of Fibershed (a nonprofit organization that develops regional fiber systems that build ecosystem and community health.) I've spent the last 15 years living in a tiny redwood forest with my husband, two ridiculous cats, a family of foxes, and myriad wildlife.

I first discovered natural dyes in 2010, when Rebecca Burgess approached me to design knitting patterns for her natural dye book *Harvesting Color*. Working with botanically dyed natural fibers and seeing the beautiful colors made from plants gathered from the surrounding landscape sparked my curiosity, and my journey with plant dyes began. Fast-forward to 2019, when I began teaching mending and slow stitching. It was then that I found a way to incorporate my love of natural dyes and plant lore into my art practice, and began hand-dyeing fabric and thread. Botanical dyes and Plant Magick both involve working with the natural world and embracing its beautiful, ever-changing, mercurial ways. They fill the gap between craft, art, and science for me—it's the alchemy of the unexplainable.

When the pandemic hit in 2020 and our regional lockdown "Shelter in Place" began, I decided to use my time exploring plants and the colors they make, with the intent to create textile art and clothing with my experiments and discoveries. During this time, California experienced an exceptional drought and three consecutive years of wildfires. The impact of this was not only visible on the landscape, but also in the colors the plants and trees were making. After two years of wet winters and significantly fewer fires, I've found that I can no longer reproduce some of those colors. Instead I have discovered new colors and found more plants to befriend. I have an ever-growing respect for land and plants, as well as their beautiful, ever-changing, mercurial ways.

I also teach natural dye and slow stitching workshops in Northern California. I enjoy sharing my knowledge of natural dyeing, Plant Magick, mending/darning, and patchwork, with a focus on minimum-waste practices. I am happiest outside, gathering madrone bark, acorns, and oak galls and experimenting with plants for dyeing.

Having the privilege of writing a book and sharing my knowledge of natural dyeing has been an incredible experience. My approach to creating color is to emphasize intent over perfection, and I hope after reading it, your love and curiosity for the land and plants that surround you grows. Remember that coaxing colors from plants requires practice, experimentation, and embracing mistakes as opportunities to learn.

Chapter 1
Mastering the Basics of Natural Dyeing

Foraging and Growing Dye Plants

I love going for a walk in nature, finding and identifying a plant, foraging, and wildcrafting colors, but it's important to remember that foraging of any kind impacts our surrounding landscape. The tips below offer a guide to gathering the abundance of nature in a mindful and respectful way, allowing us to protect the beauty of our natural world while sharing in her bounty.

MINDFUL FORAGING

Each plant contributes to our environment, providing food and shelter to insects and wildlife while nourishing the landscape. Foraging is a privilege; we are not entitled to harvest from public lands or wilderness areas. Here's a handy checklist to follow for sustainable, mindful foraging practices:

- **Don't over-harvest.** Make sure the plant is abundant. Harvest less than 20% of what is available on any particular plant, and harvest from multiple plants or locations. When gathering leaves from a tree, take every third leaf. Do not strip branches.

- **Consider the plant's lifecycle.** Never remove all of the roots, seeds, or flower heads, or take so much of the plant that it can't continue to grow and reproduce. There are some exceptions to this rule, such as harvesting invasive species. I recommend only harvesting roots from invasive plants, or cultivating the plant in your garden and maintaining careful control of its spread.

- **Never harvest any protected, endangered, or at-risk plants.** Most local land management agencies have a list of protected, endangered, or at-risk plants that you can consult before foraging.

- **Observe the health of the plant before harvesting.** Do not harvest if a plant looks sad, wilted, discolored, or overrun by pests.

- **Follow the leave-no-trace rules.** Be sure to tread lightly so as not to damage any surrounding plants, and dispose of any waste. It should look like you were never there. Respect wildlife and be considerate of other visitors to the area.

- **Harvest in the right season.** Check the best season to harvest each plant to avoid harming its lifecycle. Spring is a great time to harvest foliage and tree prunings. Summer is best for harvesting other foliage and flowers. Fall is ideal for harvesting seeds, nuts, and roots.

- **Always ask permission.** Consult the landowner or get a permit if necessary. Many wilderness areas prohibit foraging without a permit.

- **Lastly, the earth and land are precious and sacred.** Plants are not inanimate objects; they are alive, animated, and communicative. Before harvesting, take a moment to ask the plant for its permission. We are intuitive creatures and can usually tell, by a gut feeling, what the answer is. Respect the plant's wishes. Leave an offering to the plant, like water from your bottle or by sprinkling its seeds around. When we practice mindful foraging by respecting the land and developing a dialogue with our fellow nature beings, we tap into nature's magick.

SAFE FORAGING

The guidelines below will help you to stay safe while foraging for plant material:

- Start with easy-to-identify plants such as dandelion, fennel, oak galls, St. John's wort, field horsetail, bracken, and acorns.
- A good foraging book will tell you how to identify the plant as well as when and where it's likely to grow. Use books local to your region that include detailed images and descriptions. iNaturalist is an excellent phone app that you can download.
- Only harvest a plant if you are confident that you can positively identify it. Double-check multiple sources to confirm your identification.
- Make sure you have the right equipment, such as gloves, pruners, a knife, a first-aid kit, and the appropriate containers to bring the plant material home. Have water, soap, and a towel with you in case you come into contact with something that you have a reaction to. A spray bottle with rubbing alcohol and a cloth to clean pruners and scissors after cutting plant matter will help prevent the possible spreading of disease from one plant to another.
- Do not use a plant if you have a life-threatening allergy to any part of it, especially if you have a tree nut allergy.

GROWING COLOR

As well as foraging, you can find beautiful color in growing your own plants. If you have limited space, compact prolific bloomers such as marigolds, dyer's coreopsis, and dyer's chamomile are good options for growing in pots or a window box. If you have more space, weld, pericón, sulfur cosmos, and black hollyhocks are a wonderful addition to the plants listed above. If you're feeling adventurous, have lots of space, and a green thumb, things like madder, purple gromwell, safflower, dyer's alkanet, and many other herbs and flowers that produce color can be wonderful additions to any garden (see page 140 for seed sources).

Storing natural dye materials

Fresh, tender plants, leaves, and flowers should be used the day they are picked for the best results, but they can be stored in a dry, cool, dark place for up to three days. Thick, tough leaves and roots should be used within five days. Seeds, bark, and nut husks last much longer if stored in mesh bags or baskets in a dry, shady place.

If you aren't going to utilize your harvest immediately, freezing tender plants, leaves, and flowers is a great way to save them for later use.

Drying plants is another option. All you need is a food dehydrator or herb drying rack and a cool, dry space out of direct sunlight. Pay particular attention to flowers with thickly clustered petals, which tend to mold. It's also important to make sure plants are completely dry before placing them in containers for storage. Dried flowers, tree bark, cones, or onion skins can be kept in muslin or paper bags. These can then be stored in lidded tubs for added safekeeping.

Dye extracts are particularly susceptible to moisture, so I recommend adding a silica or desiccant packet to regulate moisture content and sealing in a ziplock bag. There's nothing more upsetting than discovering a batch of expensive logwood extract has solidified into a hard chunk.

Good labeling is crucial, and the more dyes and plants you accumulate, the more important this becomes. Always label your dyes with the following information: common name; Latin name; date gathered or purchased; and location or source. Keep a list of dyes and "use by dates" that you can easily reference.

Natural dyes lose potency over time. Freshly picked and dried plant material is good for up to two years, although I've found this varies from plant to plant. To avoid disappointment, I keep fabric swatches and notes on the longevity of various dyestuffs. Dyes and extracts that have been professionally processed are good for up to five years.

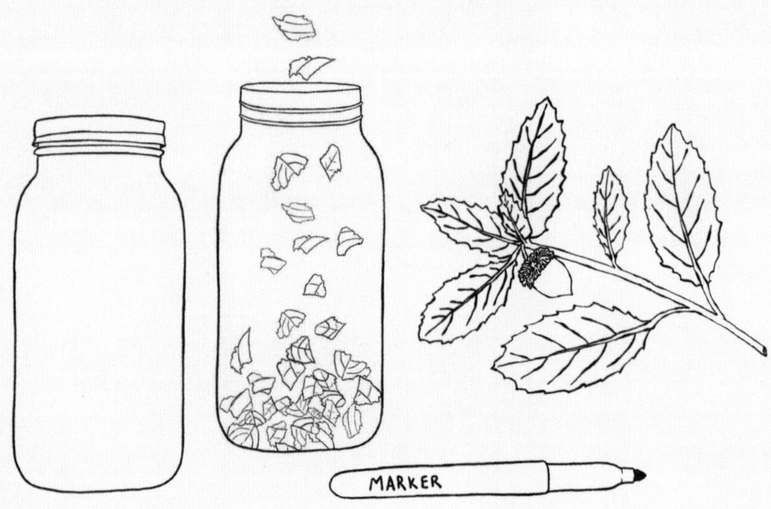

Choosing Fibers

In general, there are two groups of fiber to choose from when using natural dyes: plant (cellulose) fibers, such as cotton and linen; and protein fibers, such as wool and silk. Both groups come in a variety of natural colors, weights, and dyeables. The two groups are treated differently during the dyeing process; I use mostly silk and plant fibers in my creative process, and those will be my focus, but I will also briefly talk about wool and other animal fibers.

Plant-based vs protein-based

In the **plant-based group** there are cellulose and regenerative cellulosic fibers. Familiar examples of cellulose fibers are linen, cotton, hemp, jute, and nettle. Common regenerative fibers are rayon, modal, and lyocell. Even though regenerative fibers are made from wood pulp, the way they are manufactured means they are not truly a natural fiber, nor considered a synthetic fiber. No matter what plant fiber I'm dyeing, I always use a combination of tannin followed by aluminum acetate as a mordant to ensure better color absorption and lightfastness; I'll talk more about mordanting fibers on pages 22–35.

Protein-based fibers come from the fur/hair of animals or from the cocoons of silkworms. Wool, alpaca, mohair, and cashmere are some of the more common types. Natural dyes have an affinity to protein fibers, making them easier to dye, especially wool. Typically, aluminum sulfate or aluminum potassium sulfate is used when mordanting protein fibers. Gentle care should be used when working with animal fibers. They may felt if stirred too aggressively, boiled, or shocked with extreme temperature shifts. Aluminum triformate is a new cold-water mordant that makes dyeing protein fibers more convenient.

Top to bottom: natural linen, undyed rayon silk blend.

Color, weight, and texture

Let's think beyond white fabric. Both protein and plant fibers come in a variety of natural colors ranging from cream, oatmeal, gray, and brown. While white fabric gives you a blank slate, by choosing a naturally colored fabric you can expand your color range even further. White fabric is best suited for light colors, while using natural colored linen adds depth to medium and darker shades. I especially love using natural linen for rich jewel tones and deep grays. It's a great option if you want to avoid using iron as a modifier.

The last thing to consider is the fabric's weight and weave. Lighter-weight and more open-weave fabrics use less dye and are easier to achieve even dyeing. Heavyweight and more densely woven fabric will require more dye and take more time and tending in the dyebath. Textured fabrics that have a raised pattern or a slubby, irregular surface also take more time. Lighter-weight fabrics may appear lighter in color than heavier-weight fabrics.

If you're not familiar with different weights of fabric, gauze is the lightest and canvas is the heaviest. The weight of fabric is usually listed in ounces per square yard (oz./yd^2) or grams per square meter (GSM); the lower the number, the lighter the fabric.

Avoid using any fabric labeled "softened," "treated," or "signature finished." These fabrics have been chemically processed, which may affect the ability of mordants and natural dyes to bond to the fiber.

When dyeing garments, keep in mind that most commercial garments are sewn with polyester thread. The garment will dye, but the thread will not, so make sure to check the thread content to avoid disappointment.

FIBER	TYPE	DESCRIPTION
Linen	Plant-based (cellulose)	Linen is a strong, lightweight, bast fiber made from the flax plant, *Linum usitatissimum*. It's used to make everything from home goods to clothing. It is strong, durable, and long-lasting.
Cotton	Plant-based (cellulose)	Soft, durable fabric that is almost pure cellulose. Comes in various dyeables including woven and knitted fabrics, thread, and yarn.
Hemp	Plant-based (cellulose)	Quick-growing bast fiber that doesn't require the use of herbicides or pesticides. Hemp fabric is breathable, warm, and durable.
Nettle	Plant-based (cellulose)	Nettle cloth is a bast fiber and usually indicates fabric from the stinging nettle plant, European *Urtica dioica*.
Ramie	Plant-based (cellulose)	Ramie is a bast fiber and typically refers to China grass cloth made from white ramie (*Boehmeria nivea*) but also includes fabric made from the stems of plants in the wider nettle family.
Rayon	Plant-based (regenerative)	A smooth fabric made from regenerated cellulose from wood pulp. Includes modal and bamboo.
Lyocell	Plant-based (regenerative)	Lyocell is the third generation of regenerative fibers. TENCEL™ is the most common brand of lyocell.
Wool	Protein-based	Comes from sheep and is considered one of the easiest natural fibers to dye. Used to produce many types of textiles.
Silk	Protein-based	A natural fiber that is produced by insect larvae to create cocoons. Silk is known for being a luxurious fabric that is smooth, light, shiny, and soft.
Alpaca	Protein-based	Durable, luxurious, hypoallergenic natural fiber that comes from the hair of alpacas. Mainly used in high-end textiles.
Mohair	Protein-based	Mohair comes from angora goats. It's a luxury fiber with a high sheen and luster, and is often blended with other textiles.
Cashmere	Protein-based	A luxurious, lightweight fiber harvested from the undercoat of cashmere goats. Mainly used in high-end textiles.

PROS	CONS	COLOR
Comes in various dyeables including woven and knitted fabrics, thread, and yarn. Withstands high water temperatures. Takes natural dyes better than other plant fibers, with the exception of cotton and ramie.	Harder to achieve an even color, and the process takes a bit more patience and time.	Natural colors include light buff, oatmeal, ecru, and soft warm- and cool-toned grays. Must be bleached white.
Absorbs both mordants and dyes quicker than linen and is easier to dye. Withstands high water temperatures.	Conventional cotton is not sustainable, since it requires pesticides and uses a lot of water. Choose organic and heirloom varieties.	Natural colors range from white, cream, beige, green, mauve, and rust. The exact color depends on the plant.
Withstands high water temperatures.	Tends to dye lighter in color.	Natural colors include creamy white, brown, gray, almost black, or green. The exact color depends on the plant and how it's processed. Must be bleached white.
Withstands high water temperatures.	Does not readily accept dye.	Creamy white or very pale beige.
The strongest of the cellulose fibers and readily accepts dye. Withstands high water temperatures. Often blended with other fibers to take advantage of its unique strength, absorbency, and luster.	Expensive and can break if folded repeatedly in the same place.	Naturally white.
Inexpensive, soft, silk-like texture.	Not as environmentally friendly as lyocell. Vulnerable to high temperatures and weakens when wet.	White.
Considered to be the most environmentally friendly option; it is made in a closed-loop system that enables manufacturers to reuse 99% of the solvent used in the production process. Stronger than rayon.	Tends to dye lighter in color.	White.
Very little dye is required to create saturated, vibrant colors in a wide variety of shades and hues. Most dyes are very colorfast on wool.	Weak when wet, making it susceptible to felting. Various breeds of wool react differently when dyed. Many people are allergic to wool.	White, cream, black, brown, silver, red, and shades in between.
Can be mordanted like cellulose fibers and does not require heat in the mordanting process.	High amounts of iron will damage silk fibers. Vulnerable to high temperatures.	Color depends on the type of silkworm and the leaves it eats. Colors from domestic silkworms include white, yellow, and green.
Can be treated the same way as sheep's wool in the dyeing process, but less likely to felt.	More expensive than wool. Alpaca from older animals tends to be itchy; generally baby alpaca is the softest.	White, cream, black, brown, silver, red, and shades in between.
Very fluffy texture giving it a unique quality when dyed. Can be treated the same way as sheep's wool in the dyeing process, but less likely to felt.	People with sensitive skin find mohair itchy. Kid mohair is a softer option. Should be handled gently otherwise the fuzzy texture will become matted.	White, black, gray, brown, red, silver, charcoal, and champagne.
Very soft and has a fine halo that gives it something unique in the dyeing process.	Expensive, vulnerable to high temperatures, and difficult to care for.	White, brown, beige, and light gray.

Preparing Fibers

Once you have selected the fiber you want to work with, you will need to prepare the fabric for dyeing. Washing removes dirt, grease, and sizing, allowing mordants and dyes to deeply penetrate the fabric. Scoured items dye more evenly and are more lightfast and washfast. I recommend washing all fabrics, including those labeled "PFD" (prepared for dyeing) or "RTD" (ready to dye). Just because it looks clean doesn't mean it is clean! The method you use will depend on the type of fiber you have chosen.

How to size and cut fabric

A good habit to get into is to wash your fabric right after you purchase it, and always iron your fabric flat before cutting. This will release wrinkles and allow the fabric to lay flat, which makes it easier to cut. If you have a large piece of fabric, I suggest cutting it into 1-yard/meter lengths or fat quarters (18 x 22in/45 x 55cm US; 19 x 22in/50 x 56cm UK) first, which is a great base size to then cut into smaller pieces for testing color or using in small batch experiments for putting in dye journals (see pages 74–77).

1. You need to find (or create) one straight edge from which to cut everything else. Do this by finding the selvage edge, the finished edge on a piece of fabric that prevents it from fraying or unraveling.

2. On a hard, flat surface, use sharp scissors to cut the fabric into smaller squares or rectangles. Follow the grain line and cut the fabric in half at its midpoint horizontally, then cut it in half vertically.

Scouring plant-based fibers

Plant-based fibers are sturdy and don't need to be treated delicately like silk and other protein fibers. They can be safely scoured in a washing machine following the convenient method below, but the traditional method is useful for washing sashiko thread or yarn.

CONVENIENT METHOD

This is the method I use for most of my projects.

1. Place items into a washing machine. Wash on the longest cycle with hot water, using pH-neutral detergent. The amount of detergent used is based on the amount of fabric; use the recommended amount listed on the bottle. If your fabric seems particularly dirty, wash twice with detergent.

2. Rinse the fabric using the same setting, but this time without detergent.

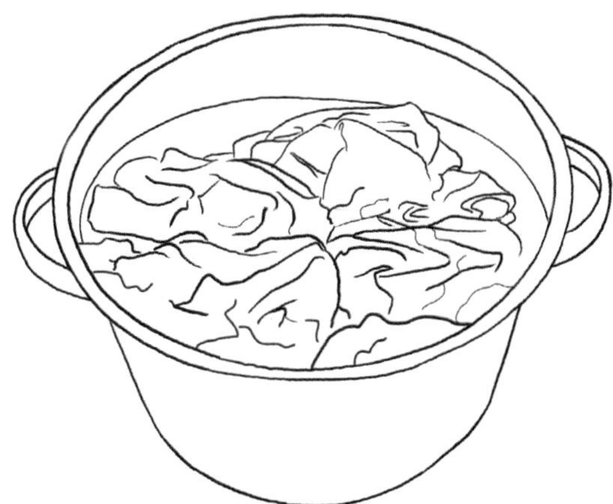

TRADITIONAL METHOD

I recommend using this method for sashiko thread or yarn.

1. Fill a large nonreactive pot with enough warm water to cover the fabric and allow it to move freely. If the fabric is tightly bunched in the water, it will not wash properly. Then add 1% weight of fiber (WOF) Synthrapol plus 1% WOF soda ash or washing soda and stir until completely dissolved.

3. Next, add the fabric and stir to remove air bubbles and make sure fabric is completely submerged. Slowly bring water to a gentle, simmering boil.

4. Maintain temperature, stirring fabric periodically. Add more water if necessary.

5. After one hour, turn off the heat, allowing the fabric to cool completely in the water. Drain water and thoroughly rinse the fabric. If the rinsing water is dark or dirty, repeat the above process.

Scouring wool

Wool and other animal fibers have a tendency to felt if stirred aggressively or exposed to extreme temperature shifts, so should not be scoured in a washing machine. Felting is when the tiny scales that make up the fibers attach and lock together. Once the fibers felt, it's irreversible. The method below is suitable for both textiles and yarn.

TRADITIONAL METHOD

1. Fill a large nonreactive pot with enough warm water to cover the fabric and allow it to move freely: If the fabric is tightly bunched in the water it will not wash properly. Add pH-neutral detergent and stir.

2. Next, add the fabric and gently stir to remove air bubbles and make sure fabric is completely submerged. Slowly bring water to 140–160°F (60–70°C). Maintain temperature, and gently rotate fabric periodically.

3. After one hour, turn off the heat and allow the fabric to cool completely in the water. Drain water and gently rinse the fabric.

4. If the rinsing water is dark or dirty, repeat the above process.

Scouring silk

Silk fibers should be treated gently. They don't contain the same contaminants as wool and lower water temperatures should be used to avoid damaging the fabric. It's safe to use a washing machine to scour most silk fabric, but if you're working with particularly delicate silk, use the bucket method below.

CONVENIENT METHOD

This method can be used for most silks.

1. Place items into a washing machine. Wash using pH-neutral detergent. The amount of detergent used is based on the amount of fabric; use the recommended amount listed on the bottle. Set the washing machine to the delicate or handwash cycle with cool or cold water.

2. Rinse the fabric using the same setting, but this time without detergent.

BUCKET METHOD

This is similar to the traditional method with the exception of water temperature.

1. Fill a large bucket or nonreactive pot with enough warm tap water (110–120°F/43–49°C) to cover the fabric and allow it to move freely. Add pH-neutral detergent and stir. The amount of detergent is based on the amount of fabric; use slightly less detergent than you would in a washing machine.

2. Add fabric and gently agitate with your hands to remove air bubbles and make sure the fabric is completely submerged. Let it soak for 10 minutes.

3. Gently agitate again then drain water and rinse the fabric. If the rinsing water is yellow or dirty, repeat the above process.

Mordants and Tannins

Mordanting is so much more than simply the process of making color stick to fabric. Mordants expand your color palette and unlock plant color possibilities, especially when you start experimenting with different tannins and tannin-plus-aluminum-salt combinations. When combining tannins and mordants, the sum is always greater than the parts.

Depending on how many natural dye books or blog posts you've read, you may already be aware that there are many different approaches to mordanting and myriad mordants and mordant recipes to explore. I've used tannins alone, aluminum salts alone, and tannin-plus-aluminum-salt combinations when mordanting plant fibers. I've also used hot-, warm-, and cool-water methods. I stopped using traditional stove-top methods after discovering how much easier it is to use a cool- or warm-water bucket method. Plus, it's more energy conscious.

I truly love clear, highly saturated, vibrant colors. In my experience, I've always achieved the best results when combining gallo tannin followed by aluminum acetate using the warm-water bucket method. If you prefer softer colors, or a simpler method, you can use tannins or aluminum salts by themselves. While aluminum acetate is the better option for mordanting cellulose fibers, especially linen, use whatever form of aluminum you are most comfortable with. There isn't a right or wrong way; it's about getting the results you want and using the method you enjoy. In this section I outline some of the methods I've used.

Top to bottom: white linen dyed with gallo tannin and aluminum acetate, satin dyed with cutch only.

Plant-based mordants and tannins

Symplocos is a new, commercially available plant-based mordant that is made from the dried fallen leaves of a deciduous tree (*Symplocos cochinchinensis*) found in Indonesia. This plant species accumulates aluminum from the soil, and other varieties of it can be found all over the world. Symplocos imparts a light yellow color to the fabric and works on both cellulose and protein fibers. If you have a plant called sweetleaf or horse-sugar (*Symplocos tinctoria*) growing in your area, consider gathering the fallen leaves and experimenting with them.

While symplocos is the only true plant-based mordant, you can also use tannins or soy milk as an alternative to aid the dyeing process. They yield softer colors and are less washfast because they have a weaker bond to the fabric. I do not have any experience with using soy milk as a pre-treatment for natural dyeing, but I use colored tannins all the time because I love the colors they yield.

While not technically mordants, tannins are worth mentioning here because they are generally used in combination with aluminum salts (see page 24) when mordanting plant-based fibers, as aluminum salts alone do not bond well with cellulose fibers. Combining tannin and aluminum can also create more vibrant, saturated colors and increase lightfastness.

Tannins can be clear or colored and, depending on what tannin you choose, they can broaden the spectrum of your color palette. The three main types of tannin are: **clear tannins (gallic)**, including gallnut, tara, and some sumacs; **yellow tannins** (ellegic), such as pomegranate, myrobalan, fustic, and some tea leaves; and **red-brown tannins (catechic)**, which include wattle, walnut hulls, cutch, quebracho, tea leaves, and some sumacs. There are so many tannins you can gather from the landscape. Every year in the late summer and early fall I gather acorns, oak galls, and black walnuts to use for mordanting and dyeing.

Unmordanted fibers dyed with cutch only. **Top to bottom**: natural linen, eucalyptus silk, wool.

Mineral salt mordants

Mineral or metallic salts have been used throughout history to create a lightfast and washfast bond between natural dyes and fibers. The most commonly used mordants come from aluminum, iron, and copper. There are many options to choose from when using aluminum, depending on what type of fiber you use. When mordanting cellulose fibers, a combination of tannin and aluminum salt will give you the most lightfast and washfast results. Tannins alone are not technically mordants but they are usually included when speaking about the mordant process for cellulose fibers, for example, "mordanted with myrobalan at 15% WOF and aluminum acetate at 5% WOF".

Aluminum is used to brighten colors; it works on both protein and plant fibers, and there are many options to choose from. **Aluminum potassium sulfate (APS)**, more commonly known as alum, has been historically used to dye protein fibers. It looks similar to salt and dissolves easily in water. **Aluminum sulfate** is like APS and gives similar results, but goes through a different refining process and is less expensive. **Aluminum acetate** is a fine powder that tends to float in the air and smells a bit like vinegar; it works exceptionally well on plant fibers. **Aluminum triformate** is a new cold-water mordant that works on all fibers. It makes animal fibers, which have a tendency to felt, more convenient to mordant.

Iron or ferrous sulfate is used to sadden colors; it's most frequently used as a post-dye or afterbath to alter the color (see page 50). It can also be used to create grays and almost black shades. Using too much iron will damage and weaken fabric. Only small amounts should be used on protein fibers. **Tin** or stannous chloride is not any more toxic than aluminum or iron. It's mostly used for creating true reds on protein fibers with cochineal. **Chrome** or potassium chromate and copper sulfate have been used in the past, but they are extremely toxic heavy metals and should never be used.

SAFETY NOTE

When people see the word "natural" they often think nontoxic or harmless, but it's always important to use common sense when working with natural dyes, mordants, and assists.

Special notes when using aluminum and iron salts:

- If ingested, seek immediate medical attention.
- When measuring iron or aluminum powder, wear a dust mask or respirator, apron, and gloves. Also, consider wearing eye protection.
- Clean any spills immediately, and wash equipment and tools promptly after use. Iron will stain surfaces, hands, and clothing. Bar Keepers Friend is a cleaning powder that removes iron/rust deposits from pots, utensils, and surfaces. It is available in grocery stores, hardware stores, and online.
- Do not allow children to use iron powder.
- Aluminum salts are considered nontoxic but still should be handled with care.

White linen dyed with tannins and aluminum acetate. **Left to right, top to bottom:** chestnut, pomegranate, sumac, gallo tannin, fustic, walnut.

Preparing to mordant

DISSOLVING TANNINS AND MORDANTS

Tannins and mordants must be dissolved prior to adding them into the mordant pot or bucket. I've found that aluminum acetate and many tannins clump when added to water, making it difficult to get them to dissolve completely. To solve this issue, when I measure out mordants I place them into heatproof glass canning jars with lids. I slowly fill the jar three-quarters full of warm water (110–120°F/43°C–49°C), I then place the lid on tight and shake vigorously for 30–60 seconds or until the powder dissolves completely. Then, I pour the contents into the pot or bucket and rinse the jar in the mordant bath.

NOTE ON TANNINS

When using extracts use 5–20% WOF, and for ground tannin plant material use 20–35% WOF. If you're hand grinding or using a spice grinder and are unable to get a powder consistency, soak the plant material for 6–12 hours to extract the tannins. For example, if I'm using oak galls that I've gathered, I'll start by breaking the galls into smaller chunks, then pour warm tap water over them until they are covered by several inches of water and allow them to soak for 12–48 hours. After soaking, strain off the liquid and use immediately for best results.

WETTING OUT FABRIC

Prior to mordanting, all fabric must be thoroughly wetted out. Fill an appropriately sized plastic bucket or nonreactive pot with enough tepid water that the fabric can move around freely. Place the fabric into the vessel and gently stir to remove air bubbles, while making sure the fabric is completely submerged.

Thin fabrics may take as little as 15–30 minutes, while thick fabrics can take eight hours or longer to become fully saturated. I usually soak thicker fabrics overnight and gently move the fabric around with my hands a couple of times during the soaking process. Plant-based fibers and silk should soak for one to four hours or overnight, and other protein fibers should soak for six to eight hours or overnight. If you're soaking canvas or heavyweight fabric, I suggest 12–24 hours, or even running it through a long wash cycle without detergent to make sure it is thoroughly wetted through.

Before removing your fabric, double-check to make sure it is evenly saturated. When you are ready, remove the fabric from the vessel and gently squeeze out any excess water. Open the fabric up and place it into the mordanting vessel.

Mordanting methods

There are two basic methods for mordanting: the warm-/cool-water bucket method; and the traditional hot-water stove-top method. One method isn't better than the other. Heating the solution—as is done in the stove-top method—simply accelerates the mordanting process. I prefer using the warm-water bucket method for plant fibers, and the cold-water bucket method using aluminum triformate for protein fibers. This style of mordanting allows me to multitask and be more productive with my time.

The recipes below are meant to be flexible and customizable, so you can adjust and experiment to find the perfect balance for your creative practice. You'll use the same equipment for each of the recipes. If any additional equipment is required, it will be listed as special equipment.

EQUIPMENT NEEDED

- One 3–5-gallon (11–19-liter) bucket with lid or large nonreactive pot with lid. (Use a smaller vessel if you only plan on mordanting small amounts [1oz/30g] of fabric.)
- Additional bucket (for rinsing)
- Nonreactive large spoon or tongs
- Small jars with lids
- Instant-read digital thermometer
- Household gloves
- N-95 or similar particle mask
- Apron
- Towel
- Timer

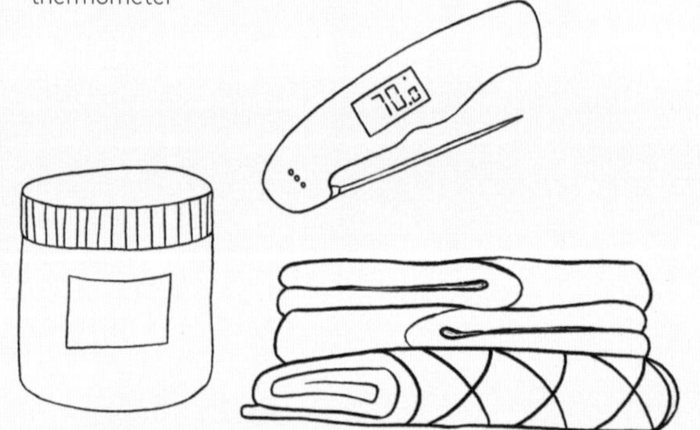

WARM-WATER BUCKET METHOD

This method is best suited for plant-based fibers. I like to be energy conscious, so I cover the buckets with several towels and/or a wool blanket to insulate the buckets and help maintain the temperature. This minimizes the need to reheat water.

SPECIAL EQUIPMENT

- Additional 3–5-gallon (11–19-liter) bucket with lid or large nonreactive pot with lid. (Use a smaller vessel if you only plan on mordanting small amounts [1oz/30g] of fabric.)
- Several towels or a wool blanket for insulating

COMPONENTS

- Tannin of choice, 5–20% WOF; 5% to increase lightfastness, 10% to increase lightfastness and color saturation, and 15–20% to impart more base color if using a colored tannin.
- Aluminum salt of choice
- Aluminum acetate: 5–8% WOF
- Aluminum sulfate or aluminum potassium sulfate, 15–20% WOF, plus soda ash, 2% WOF (You can skip the soda ash if you like, though the aluminum sulfate or aluminum potassium sulfate may not bond as strongly to the fabric. I've also read that soda ash can make linen feel rough.)

WATER TEMPERATURE

115–120°F/46–49°C

SOAKING TIMES

Two to three hours for a tannin bath and an additional one to two hours for the aluminum salt bath. The above are suggested times, but you can leave the fabric to soak for longer or overnight. It is okay if the water cools off during the mordanting process.

STAGE 1: CREATING A TANNIN BATH

1. First, completely dissolve the tannin of choice in a separate jar. Fill one of the buckets halfway with warm water (115–120°F/46–49°C). Next, add the tannin solution to the bucket, swish the jar in the water to remove any leftover tannin, and stir. Add enough additional warm water to allow the fabric to move freely.

2. Add the fabric to the bucket and gently rotate to remove air bubbles while making sure the fabric is completely submerged. Add additional warm water if needed. Cover the bucket with a lid. Revisit the bucket and gently rotate the fabric every 20–30 minutes. I prefer to rotate the fabric with my hands (wearing household gloves), as it allows for a more even rotation, but you can also rotate the fabric with a nonreactive spoon or tongs.

3. Once the fabric has soaked, remove and squeeze the excess tannin back into the bucket. Save the tannin solution and use it again, if desired (see page 34).

4. Gently rinse the tannin-soaked fabric in a bucket of cold water to remove any residue or grit. Mordant the fabric right away while still damp for best results.

SAFETY NOTE

An N-95 or high-grade particle mask and household gloves should always be worn whenever handling powders and making solutions. Household gloves should also be worn anytime you have contact with solutions, especially when handling textiles.

STAGE 2: CREATING AN ALUMINUM SALT BATH

1. If using aluminum acetate: First, completely dissolve the aluminum acetate in a jar with warm water. Fill one of the buckets halfway with warm water (115–120°F/46–49°C). Add the solution to the bucket and swish the jar in the water to remove any leftover solution.

If using aluminum potassium sulfate or aluminum sulfate: First, completely dissolve the aluminum potassium sulfate or aluminum sulfate in a jar with warm water (115–120°F/46–49°C). Fill one of the buckets halfway with warm water. Add the solution to the bucket, swish the jar in the water to remove any leftover solution. Next, in a separate jar dissolve the soda ash in warm water and add to the bucket and stir. The solution will bubble up. This is normal and harmless, carbon dioxide is being released. Wait for the bubbles to subside. Add enough additional water to allow the fabric to move freely.

2. Add the fabric to the bucket and gently stir to remove air bubbles while making sure the fabric is completely submerged. Add more warm water if needed. Cover the bucket with a lid. Revisit the bucket and gently rotate the fabric every 20–30 minutes.

3. Once the fabric has soaked, remove and squeeze the excess mordant back into the bucket. Save the mordant solution and use it again, if desired (see page 34).

4. Gently rinse the mordanted fabric in a bucket of cold water to remove any residual aluminum salt. Either dye immediately or line dry.

SIMPLY TANNIN

This method can be used on both cellulose and protein fibers, and is a good method if you prefer muted colors. There are many leaves that give beautiful soft pinks, but when mordanted with aluminum salts, they shift to yellow. If I want to avoid this, I will mordant with a clear tannin like gallo or tara. The main drawback of using tannins alone to mordant, is that the fabric may be less light- and washfast.

COMPONENTS

- Tannin of choice, 5–15% WOF

WATER TEMPERATURE

115–120°F/46–49°C

SOAKING TIMES

Four to eight hours, or overnight for best results.

1. First, completely dissolve the tannin of choice in a jar. Fill the bucket halfway with warm water (115–120°F/46–49°C). Next, add the tannin solution to the bucket, swish the jar in the water to remove any leftover tannin, and stir. Add enough additional warm water to allow the fabric to move freely.

2. Add the fabric to the bucket and gently rotate to remove air bubbles, while making sure the fabric is completely submerged. Add additional warm water if needed. Cover the bucket with a lid. Revisit the bucket and gently rotate the fabric every 45–60 minutes.

3. Once the fabric has soaked, remove and squeeze the excess tannin back into the bucket. Save the tannin solution and use it again, if desired (see page 34).

4. Gently rinse the tannin-soaked fabric in a bucket of cold water to remove any residue or grit. For best results dye the fabric right away.

ALUMINUM ACETATE AND CHALK BATH

This method tends to yield a less lightfast and less saturated color. Fabric mordanted with aluminum acetate alone must be fixed with a chalk afterbath before dyeing. This removes excess mordant and ensures a more evenly dyed fabric.

SPECIAL EQUIPMENT

- Bucket for chalk afterbath

COMPONENTS

- Aluminum acetate, 8–10% WOF
- Chalk (calcium carbonate), 5% WOF

WATER TEMPERATURE

115–120°F/46–49°C

SOAKING TIMES

One to two hours.

1. First, completely dissolve aluminum acetate in a jar with warm water. Fill the bucket halfway with warm water (115–120°F/46–49°C). Next, add the solution to the bucket, swish the jar in the water to remove any leftover solution, and stir. Add enough additional warm water to allow the fabric to move freely.

2. Add the fabric to the bucket and gently stir to remove air bubbles, while making sure the fabric is completely submerged. Add more warm water if needed. Cover the bucket with a lid. Revisit the bucket and gently rotate the fabric every 20–30 minutes. I prefer to rotate the fabric with my hands (wearing household gloves), as it allows for a more even rotation, but you can also rotate the fabric with a nonreactive spoon or tongs.

3. Once the fabric is done soaking, remove and squeeze the excess mordant back into the bucket. Save the mordant solution and use it again if desired (see page 34).

4. Gently rinse the mordanted fabric in a bucket of cold water to remove any residual aluminum acetate.

5. Make the chalk solution by mixing the calcium carbonate with warm water in a jar until dissolved. Fill a bucket halfway with warm water, add the chalk solution, and stir.

6. Next, add the mordanted fabric to the bucket and gently stir to remove air bubbles, while making sure the fabric is completely submerged. Add more warm water if needed. Let the fabric soak for 10–15 minutes. Rotate the fabric gently after five minutes.

7. Once the fabric has soaked, remove and squeeze the excess chalk solution back into the bucket. Thoroughly rinse the fabric in clean cold water. Discard chalk solution. Dye immediately or line dry.

COOL-WATER METHOD USING ALUMINUM TRIFORMATE

This method is best suited for protein fibers. It eliminates the risk of felting wool or damaging delicate silk by prolonged exposure to high temperatures.

SPECIAL EQUIPMENT

- Bucket or nonreactive pot for chalk solution

COMPONENTS

- Aluminum triformate, 5–10% WOF

WATER TEMPERATURE

90–110°F/32–43°C

SOAKING TIMES

Three to four hours for light colors; five to eight hours for medium, and 12–24 hours for dark colors: 24 hours yields the best results.

1. First, dissolve aluminum triformate in a separate jar. Fill the bucket or nonreactive pot halfway with tepid water (90–110°F/32–43°C). Next, add the solution to the bucket, swish the jar in the water to remove any leftover solution, and stir. Add enough additional tepid water to allow the fabric to move freely.

2. Add the fabric to the bucket or pot and gently stir to remove air bubbles, making sure the fabric is completely submerged. Add more water if needed. Cover the bucket or pot with a lid, gently rotating the fabric once an hour. If soaking fabric for longer lengths of time rotate every couple of hours. I prefer to rotate the fabric with my hands (wearing household gloves), but you can also use a nonreactive spoon or tongs.

3. Once the fabric has soaked, remove and squeeze the excess mordant back into the bucket or pot. Save the mordant solution and use it again, if desired (see page 34).

4. Gently rinse the mordanted fabric in a bucket of cool water. Either dye immediately or line dry.

TRADITIONAL HEATED METHOD USING ALUMINUM POTASSIUM SULFATE

This method can be used on all fibers. The important thing to remember when working with wool or animal fibers is not to be overly aggressive when stirring or squeezing liquid from the fabric. I do not recommend this method for silk.

SPECIAL EQUIPMENT

- Heat source
- Large nonreactive pots with lids
- Pot holders

COMPONENTS

- For animal fibers: Aluminum potassium sulfate, 15% WOF
- For plant-based fibers: Aluminum potassium sulfate, 15% WOF, plus soda ash, 2% WOF (You can skip the soda ash if you like, though the aluminum potassium sulfate may not bond as strongly to the fabric. I've also read that it can make linen feel rough.)

WATER TEMPERATURE

Start with tepid tap water (90–110°F/32–43°C)

SOAKING TIME

60 minutes

1. If using animal fibers: First, completely dissolve the aluminum potassium sulfate in a jar with warm water. Next, fill the pot halfway with tepid water. Add the solution to the pot, swish the jar in the water to remove any leftover solution, and stir. Add enough additional water to allow the fabric to move freely.

If using plant fibers: First, completely dissolve the aluminum potassium sulfate in a jar with warm water. Next, dissolve the soda ash in a separate jar with warm/hot water. Fill the pot halfway with tepid water. Add the aluminum potassium sulfate solution to the pot, swish the jar in the water to remove any leftover solution, then add the soda ash solution to the pot and stir. The combined solutions will bubble up. This is normal and harmless; carbon dioxide is being released. Wait for the bubbles to subside. Add enough additional water to allow the fabric to move freely.

2. Add the fabric and gently stir to remove air bubbles, while making sure it is completely submerged. Add more warm water if needed. Cover the pot with a lid. Slowly, over the course of 30 minutes, bring the water up to 190°F (88°C) and maintain the temperature for 60 minutes. Revisit the pot every 15 minutes and gently rotate the fabric using a nonreactive spoon or tongs. Make sure the fabric stays submerged and that the mordant bath doesn't come to a boil.

3. After 60 minutes, turn off the heat and remove the lid. Allow the fabric to cool. Once cooled, remove the fabric and gently squeeze the excess mordant back into the pot.

4. Gently rinse the mordanted fabric in cool water. Dye immediately or line dry. Once the fabric is completely dried, store indoors in a cool, dry place in a labeled, lidded container or bag for later use. It's important to protect it from dust and other contaminants.

SAFETY NOTE

If you are working indoors, it is important to have good ventilation. Make sure to use an exhaust fan and open some windows. It is also recommended to wear a mask to avoid breathing in steam/fumes. Even if working outside, avoid breathing in steam/fumes.

Finishing up

DISPOSAL

Exhausted mordant baths of aluminum, iron, or tannins may be safely disposed of in a municipal water system by diluting them and pouring them down the drain. To be extra safe, you can add one teaspoon of washing soda to the solution to neutralize it before disposing of it. Do not pour the solution down the drain if you have a septic system. Do not dispose of exhausted baths in waterways, rivers, or storm drains. If you have a garden, dilute the mordant and pour it onto the soil of acid-loving plants like hydrangeas, azaleas, camellias, rhododendrons, and magnolias. You can pour diluted iron water onto the ground; I use it to water curly dock because this plant has the ability to absorb iron from the ground. I then harvest the roots for natural dyeing, and I think you get a better color this way.

REUSING MORDANT BATHS

This saves water and aluminum salts; I reuse my mordant baths anywhere from two to four times. Simply reheat the water to the desired temperature and recharge the bath with 25–50% of the amount of required tannin or aluminum salt to the vessel (for example if the original amount was 10g of aluminum acetate, you would add 2.5–5g to recharge). If the mordant bath accumulates a lot of sediment, discard it and start over. Sediment is usually the result of not rinsing the fabric thoroughly between the tannin application and the mordant bath. If using aluminum acetate, it may become a little cloudy with repeated use, especially if you have hard water. Give it a good stir, it's still good to use.

The Folk Method

The folk method is one of the simplest ways to explore natural colors from your landscape and discover plants that you can use for natural dyeing. It's based on the folk method of medicine-making and doesn't use specific measurements, only parts. This means there is no difficult math involved and you don't need to meticulously weigh everything, with the exception of mordants. As you grow as a natural dyer, you will eventually rely on your intuition and knowledge to craft color.

The folk method is best suited for plants that you gather or grow, rather than expensive natural dye extracts or raw dye material purchased online from a natural dye supplier. When using this method there may be more variation from bath to bath. It's a good idea to keep fabric swatches and notes in your dye journal (see pages 74–77) because results from foraged plants can differ depending on the time of year gathered, soil type, climate, and weather. I like to think of it as: plant magick + earth magick + forest magick = a kaleidoscope of colors.

The folk-method process is similar to the ratio method of immersion dyeing (see pages 42–46). The main difference is that proportions are used instead of percentages based on the weight of material to be dyed (known as the weight of fiber or WOF). The main difference is the folk method uses foraged plant matter. If I'm dyeing with dried flowers or walnut husks, I'll use the recommended percentage based on WOF.

The amount of fabric and range of color you can dye using this method is based on the type of plant, if it produces gentle or strong color, and the amount of plant matter that has been gathered. There is no set answer to this. You develop a general idea after you've worked with several different plants. Most plants benefit from soaking in cool water for several hours or overnight before heating. Some plants need coaxing, while others begin to yield color in minutes. I always start by making a test jar. If all my samples have a strong color and the remaining liquid in the jar still has a strong color, I'll dye a 12-in (30-cm) square of fabric. I'll compare the color to the swatches and observe what the remaining liquid looks like. I may dye another piece of fabric if the liquid still has a strong to medium color. Based on my observations, I'll note general plant-to-fabric proportions in my journal.

Making a folk-method dyebath

PREPPING PLANT MATTER

After gathering, gently shake all plant matter to remove any bugs or loose dirt. Leaves, bark, seeds, acorns, and cones should be soaked for a short time and rinsed to remove any surface grime. Nut husks and redwood cones can be gently wiped to remove any surface dirt. Redwood cones should be handled with care when gathered and processed—the young green cones are sturdy, however the dry, fresh cones contain a glitter-like pigment that falls out when tapped. The cone itself also contains pigment but in less quantity.

METHOD 1

1. The proportions are simple: Fill a pot a third or just under half full with processed plant matter. Then fill the pot two-thirds full of water.

2. Heat pot to the recommended temperature based on the type of plant matter (see pages 38–40).

3. Once at temperature, either lower the heat to maintain the temperature or remove the dyebath from the heat and wrap it with several cotton towels or a wool blanket to insulate the pot and save energy. If I'm using small dyebaths, I'll wrap them first and then place them in a cardboard box. For larger pots, I place a cardboard box over the top after wrapping the pot.

4. Maintain temperature for between 45 minutes to two hours, or until the dyebath has developed a good color. Consult your dye journal if needed. I always place a small fabric sample in the pot and use this to gauge how the dyebath is developing.

5. Once the dyebath has developed good color, strain or remove the plant matter.

METHOD 2

1. Fill the dyebath two-thirds full with water. Place the dyestuff into a mesh or muslin bag, bring the water up to the appropriate temperature (see pages 38–40) and steep like tea.

2. Remove the bag of dyestuff from the dyebath after the required amount of time or once the dyebath has developed good color. Turn off the heat and let the bag cool until it's safe to handle. When sufficiently cool, wearing gloves, squeeze any extra liquid out of the bag and return this liquid to the dyebath.

DYEING WITH FLOWERS

Water temperature: 140–160°F/60–71°C
Extraction time: 45–60 minutes

Flowers should be used in their whole form. Whether dried or fresh, they don't require soaking before extraction. Most flowers produce clear, bright colors if they are processed for shorter periods of time at lower temperatures. Once the dyebath is saturated with pigment, strain out the flowers to get the best results. If the temperature goes over for a short period of time, don't worry, it's not ruined, but the colors might not be as vivid or may shift. Boiling may result in murky, dull colors.

DYEING WITH PLANT AND TREE LEAVES

Water temperature: 180°F/82°C
Extraction time: One to three hours. Thicker leaves will take two to three hours.

Fresh leaves should be soaked for one to two hours, or overnight. If using **dried leaves**, such as loquat, allow to soak overnight. You can use cold water or pour 180°F (82°C) water over them to speed up the process.

In the dyebath, maintain a temperature of 180°F (82°C) for one to two hours. There are exceptions where higher temperatures are needed and longer steeping times. I love the shade of blue that gum eucalyptus leaves make when rapidly simmered or gently boiled at 205°F (96°C) for an additional 45 minutes.

DYEING WITH SEED PODS, CONES, ACORNS, OAK GALLS, AND NUT HUSKS

Water temperature: 180–190°F (82–88°C)
Extraction time: Two to three hours, or up to three days. Extraction times vary depending on the type of material used. I add a fabric sample to test the color strength. I'll gently boil a small test batch to see what happens.

I usually leave **seed pods** and **cones** whole, unless they are large, in which case I'll break them open or into smaller pieces. I then soak them overnight in cold water, or pour 180°F (82°C) water over them to speed up the process. **Redwood cones** are the one exception since, they yield color in seconds or minutes in cold water. A strong dyebath can take as little as 45 minutes when heated. If they've been out in the elements, this may take a bit longer. If they are old or have been rained on several times, there will be little to no pigment left.

Acorns and **walnuts** with green husks should be cracked open or broken in half; this can be done by stepping on them or using a hammer or rock. I usually use a 3-lb (1.3-kg) mini sledgehammer or the flat side of a hammer. Just make sure the hammer isn't rusty. **Dried walnut** or **other nut husks** can be flaked or scraped off, or soaked whole. Always wear gloves when working with walnuts, otherwise they will stain your hands. **Green walnuts** give a stronger color than dried husks as they are higher in tannins. **Oak galls** should be broken into smaller pieces or ground up. The smaller the pieces, the shorter the soaking time.

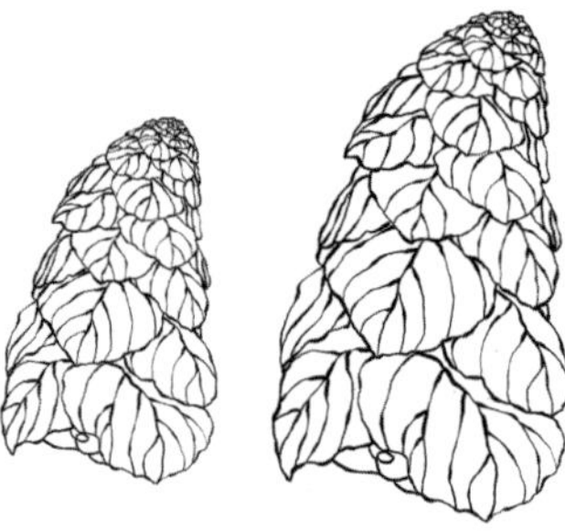

DYEING WITH SAWDUST, WOOD CHIPS, BARK, AND ROOTS

Water temperature for sawdust/woodchips: 180–190°F (80–87°C)
Extraction time: One to two hours

Water temperature for bark/roots: 190–205°F (87–96°C)
Extraction time: Much like acorns and nut husks, extraction times vary depending on the type of material used. I always add a fabric sample to the dyebath to test the color strength. If you're happy with the color extracted from soaking for several days, you can remove the dyestuff and use the liquid without further heating. I'll often make several dyebaths from the same bark; shorter and longer soaking times can yield a wonderful range of color. I'll also gently boil a small test batch to see what happens.

Bark, **woodchips**, and **roots** should be soaked in cold water overnight or for several days, and sometimes up to a week, to develop rich colors. This can be heated periodically to speed up the extraction. Avoid boiling tannin-rich bark and sawdust as the tannins can over-oxidize and you may lose brighter, clearer colors. **Cherry bark** yields soft, clear peaches and richer, pinky corals with longer soaking times, but they shift more toward tan when boiled. Most roots and bark can be dried and reused until all the pigment has been extracted.

For **fine sawdust**, cover in water or place into a mesh or muslin bag, and let it soak for four hours or overnight. It will settle to the bottom when it's ready.

DYEING WITH MUSHROOMS

Dyeing with mushrooms has more variables depending on the species used. I suggest taking a class or reaching out to your local mycology association.

Correct identification of mushrooms is crucial. The dyeball mushroom (see page 124), is a good beginner mushroom to experiment with as they're easy to identify and process. I strongly recommend processing this mushroom outside; the powdery spores are easily airborne. Gloves and a dust mask should always be worn while processing the dyeball mushroom.

If the mushroom is dried, treat it like a dye extract:

1. Gently crumble the desired amount of the mushroom into a jar, add a few drops of dish soap or a teaspoon of vegetable glycerine, then slowly add boiling water leaving some room at the top. The spores will float on the surface. The dried spores are water-soluble but water-resistant. Adding dish soap or glycerine will help the spores dissolve more quickly.

2. Place the lid on the jar and tighten, then shake the jar vigorously. The spores will begin to dissolve. I leave the solution to soak for a few days, shaking the jar twice daily.

3. Once it looks dissolved, it's ready to use. If the mushroom is still moist, break or cut it into smaller pieces. Add it to your dyebath with a few drops of dish soap or a teaspoon of vegetable glycerine.

4. Heat the dyebath to a temperature of 180–205°F. This can be simmered for one to two hours, or until the mushroom looks fully dissolved. Alternatively, bring the bath to temperature then turn off the heat and cover. Allow to steep for two to four hours.

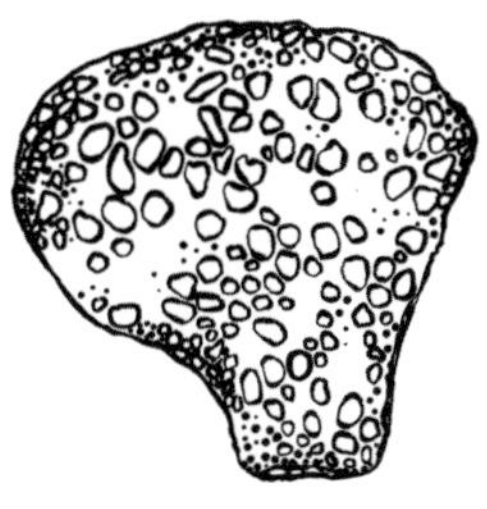

Preparing and dyeing fabric

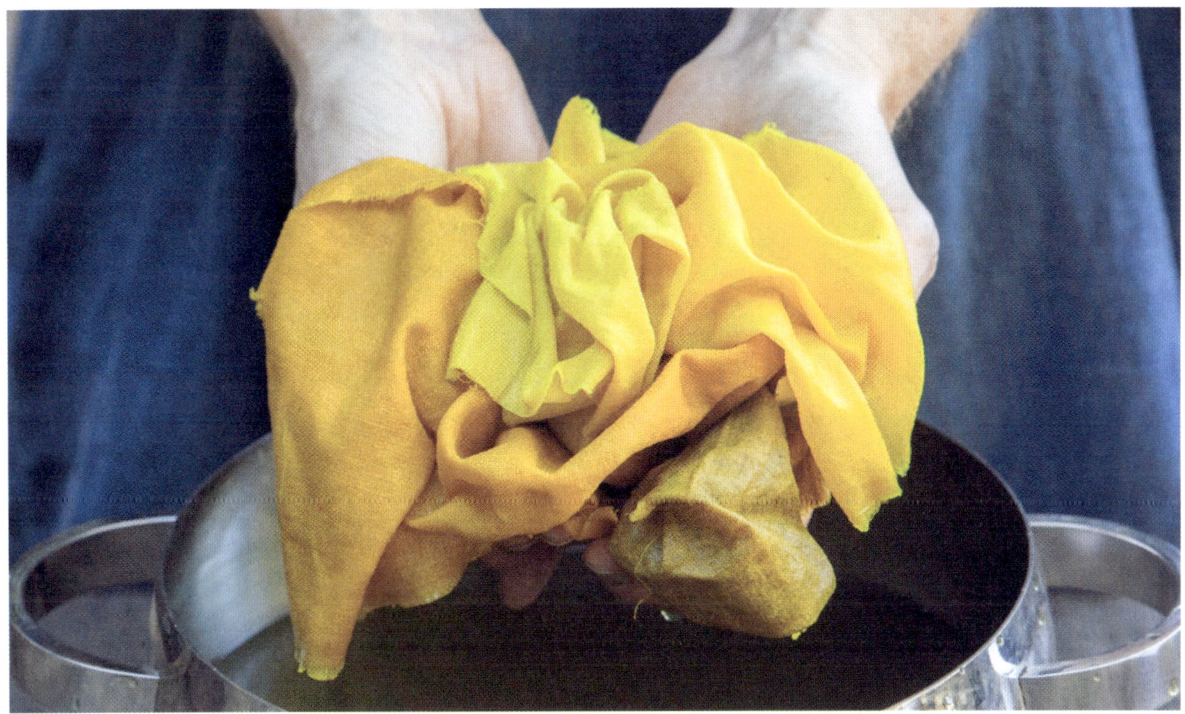

PREPARING FABRIC

Your fiber should be scoured and mordanted, if needed, prior to dyeing. Soak the fabric and thoroughly wet it out in water.

DYEING FABRIC

1. Remove the soaking fabric from the water and gently wring out. Open the fabric up completely and lower it vertically into the dyebath. Stir to remove any air bubbles, making sure the fabric is fully submerged. Rotate the fabric periodically so that it dyes evenly. Make sure fabric can move freely and don't overcrowd the dyebath.

2. After 30 minutes to four hours, or after achieving the desired color, remove the fabric from the dyebath or turn off the heat and allow the fabric to cool in the dyebath. Leaving the fabric in the dyebath may result in a stronger color.

3. Once all the fabric is dyed and it's cool enough to handle, gently rinse the dyed goods to make sure there is no residual dye, then wash gently with pH-neutral soap. This can be done by hand, or in a washing machine using cold water and a gentle cycle. Air dry out of direct sunlight. If you're rinsing different batches of fabric, start with the lightest color, moving onto darker colors to save water. Remember to wash like colors together, and always follow the manufacturer's care instructions for the fabric.

Traditional Ratio Method

Unlike the folk method, the ratio method uses specific weights of dyestuff and fabric. Dry fabric is weighed and a specific amount of dyestuff or extract is calculated based on the weight of fabric (WOF). The dye is extracted in a heated water bath. This is very straightforward, but there are still variations from bath to bath, especially if you buy your dyestuff from different sources. For the most consistent results, you should always buy from the same source, do a test swatch, and record the results in your dye journal (see pages 74–77).

Preparing the dyestuff

For this method, I was taught to soak everything overnight in cool water first to help extract more color and yield a richer dyebath. I'm not sure if it is always necessary, or if it has just become part of my ritual. There is a lot of natural dye lore, and all teachers and books have their own methods. In spite of the sometimes conflicting information out there, there is no right or wrong approach—do what you feel works best for you.

RAW DYESTUFF

Dye plants can come in several forms when purchased from a retailer:

- **Whole dried plants** must be broken or cut into smaller pieces, except whole flowers or petals.
- **Whole roots** should be chopped and ground.
- **Whole cochineal bugs** can be ground with a mortar and pestle, or placed in a coffee grinder and ground into a powder. I extract pigment from ground cochineal in a small heatproof container, treating it like a dye extract. Discard the sediment after straining.
- **Ground plants** can be used as is.
- **Powdered dye extracts** have already been processed into pure pigment in a controlled laboratory and need to be dissolved in water.
- **Purple gromwell (shikon) and dyer's alkanet** are not water-soluble and need to be extracted by soaking them in rubbing alcohol or vodka (see page 44).

NON WATER-SOLUBLE PIGMENT

There are two non water-soluble pigments mentioned in this book: purple gromwell (see page 90) and dyer's alkanet (see page 85). Both produce gray tones when extracted with water alone.

To extract the purple pigment: Place the desired amount of powder into a glass jar with a lid. Pour enough clear rubbing alcohol or vodka over the powder to form a thin syrupy liquid. Cover the jar with a lid and let it sit at room temperature for several days to extract the color. When the liquid has developed a strong color, pour it through a fine-mesh strainer and into a clean glass jar. It is now ready to use. This solution should always be added to water and diluted before heating to 120°F (48°C) for purple gromwell and 140°F (60°C) for dyer's alkanet. Avoid open flames, as the alcohol may be flammable if insufficiently diluted.

DYE EXTRACTS

I recommend dissolving dye extracts in a small heatproof container, such as a glass jar with a lid, instead of trying to dissolve them in the dyebath.

1. Place the recommended amount of dye extract into a heatproof container, then pour a small amount of warm water (120°F/48°C) to wet out the powder and stir to form a loose paste.

2. Add enough warm water to create a concentrated solution. Place the lid onto the jar and tighten. Give it a good shake and make sure the extract is fully dissolved before pouring it through a fine-mesh strainer and into the dyebath.

Some dye extracts, such as **cutch**, will get quite sticky and tend to form lumps. Let these dyes sit for several hours or overnight, and they will be easier to dissolve. If you've let the solution sit for a few hours or overnight, give it a good shake or stir before pouring through a fine-mesh strainer. If there are any lumps of undissolved extract, use the back of a spoon to push them through the strainer and rinse any residual extract in the dyebath.

PROCESSING DYESTUFFS FOR THE RATIO METHOD

Water temperature for flowers: 140–160°F (60–71°C)
Extraction time: 45–60 minutes (except for safflower)

Water temperature for plants: 180–190°F (80–87°C)
Extraction time: 45–60 minutes

Water temperature for sawdust: 180–190°F (80-87°C)
Extraction time: 1–2 hours

Water temperature for madder root: 150°F (65°C)
Extraction time: 2 hours

There are two ways extract pigment:

METHOD 1

1. Place the dyestuff directly into the dye pot and fill two-thirds full with water. Bring the water to temperature, stirring the pot periodically.

2. After the required amount of time or once the dyebath has developed a good color, turn off the heat, allow to cool until the pot is safe to handle, and strain out the dyestuffs.

METHOD 2

1. Fill the dyebath two-thirds full with water. Place dyestuff into a mesh or muslin bag, bring the water up to the appropriate temperature and steep like tea.

2. Remove the bag of dyestuff from the dyebath after the required amount of time or once the dyebath has developed good color. Turn off the heat and let the bag cool until it's safe to handle. When sufficiently cool, wearing gloves, squeeze any extra liquid out of the bag and return this liquid to the dyebath.

Preparing fabric and making the dyebath

PREPARING FABRIC

Your fiber should be scoured and mordanted (if needed) prior to dyeing. Calculate the amount of dye you need by weighing the dry fabric you want to dye. This measurement is known as the weight of fiber or WOF. The amount of dye that you need is then calculated as a percentage of the WOF. After calculating the amount of dye, soak the fabric and wet it out.

PREPARING THE DYEBATH

1. The first step in preparing the dyebath for the ratio method is to calculate the amount of dyestuff required. Once you've selected your dyestuff, and decided if you want a light, medium, or dark color, you can calculate the percentage needed based on the WOF. Weigh out the required amount of dyestuff and set aside.

2. If you have a prepared dyebath, top it up with fresh water if necessary. Add the dyestuff and heat the dyebath gradually until it reaches the required temperature. Follow the guidelines below for madder, cochineal, and dye extracts.

Ground madder and munjeet root should be heated slowly, similar to a dye extract. Gradually bring the dyebath up to 150°F (65°C) over the course of an hour, then maintain the dyebath at this temperature for another hour. Strain out the madder. You can also use a mesh or muslin bag to place the ground madder or munjeet root in, which is easier then straining.

If you're using an **extract or a cochineal solution**, strain it through a fine-mesh strainer into a pot filled two-thirds with water. Start heating the water and bring to a temperature of about 90°F (33°C). Hold at this warm temperature for 30 minutes. Next, bring the temperature up gradually to 180°F (80°C).

Dyeing fabric

1. Remove the soaking fabric from the water and gently wring out. Open up the fabric completely and lower it vertically into the dyebath. Stir to remove any air bubbles, making sure the fabric is fully submerged. Rotate the fabric periodically so that it dyes evenly. Make sure fabric can move freely and don't overcrowd the dyebath.

2. After 30–60 minutes, or once the desired color is achieved, remove the fabric from the dyebath or turn off the heat and allow the fabric to cool in the dyebath.

3. Once all the fabric is dyed and it's cool enough to handle, gently rinse the dyed goods to make sure there is no residual dye, then wash gently with pH-neutral soap. This can be done by hand or in a washing machine using cold water and a gentle cycle. Air dry out of direct sunlight. If you're rinsing different batches of fabric, start with the lightest color, moving onto darker colors to save water. Remember to wash like colors together, and always follow the manufacturer's care instructions for the fabric.

Modifiers and Color Changers

After you've mordanted and dyed your fiber, you can widen the spectrum of colors further by using modifiers to shift them, or sometimes even change them entirely. While modifiers are usually applied directly after dyeing, they can also be used on fabric that has already been dried and put away. I recommend keeping a swatch of the original color along with the modified color in your dye journal (see pages 74–77), adding notes and observations, plus testing a small swatch and recording results before modifying larger pieces of fabric.

Acid and alkaline modifiers

Shifting the pH of a dye using acid or alkaline modifiers is one way to expand your color palette. An acidic or alkaline modifier can be added directly to a dyebath or a separate afterbath can be made. A separate afterbath will give more control over the shift in color and the dyebath will be preserved so you can continue to use it. You can modify fabric that has already been washed and dried, the fabric will just need to be wetted out.

Keep in mind that some dyes are more sensitive to pH than others. Alkaline modifiers—like baking soda, baking powder, washing soda, and soda ash—may change colors in a variety of ways. Most often, they shift purples and pinks toward blue, or yellows and reds toward pink.

Acid modifiers—like vinegar, lemon or lime juice, and citric acid—shift colors toward reds, oranges, yellows, and pinks depending on the natural dye used.

ADJUSTING COLOR WITH A PH AFTERBATH

EQUIPMENT NEEDED

- pH strips
- Measuring spoon
- Nonreactive vessel
- Gloves
- Modifier of choice

1. Fill a nonreactive vessel with warm water and test the pH using a pH strip. (Using warmer water will accelerate the process. When using an acid modifier, I like using cooler water because it gives me more control over the shift in color.)

2. Add a small amount of your chosen modifier—1 tsp (6g) per gallon (3 liters) of water is a good starting measurement—and stir until completely incorporated or dissolved. Check the pH again and add enough modifier to shift water to the desired pH level: for alkaline baths between 9–11 is best, and for acid baths between 3–5.

3. Place the fabric into the bath and gently stir to remove air bubbles, making sure the fabric is completely submerged.

4. Remove fabric when the desired color is achieved. Thoroughly rinse the fabric with water, then wash with pH-neutral soap.

Mineral salts as modifiers

Iron and copper both tend to darken colors; copper is used to shift colors toward green or brown, while iron is used to dull, deepen, or shift colors toward shades of gray and almost black. Iron is by far my favorite modifier to use: yellows transform into chartreuse and olive greens, while reds and pinks become mauves and purply hues.

You can use mineral salts in the powder form or from metal scraps. Copper, in the form of copper sulfate, is toxic and should never be used, so I recommend leaching it out of copper/brass vessels or metal scraps by adding them to a stainless steel pot with slightly acidic water. The fabric absorbs all the copper extracted from the scraps and no residual copper is left in the water. When using iron, remember that a little goes a long way and as such it should be used sparingly, especially on protein fibers and in particular silk. Too much iron will damage the fiber and cause it to become brittle. Both copper and iron afterbaths will increase lightfastness.

Both of the following methods work well on plant or protein fibers. I recommend using designated tools and a nonreactive pot, especially when using iron. There is nothing worse than residual iron contaminating a future dyebath. Always wear a mask when working with powders. Before proceeding, please see the safety and disposal guidelines on pages 56–57.

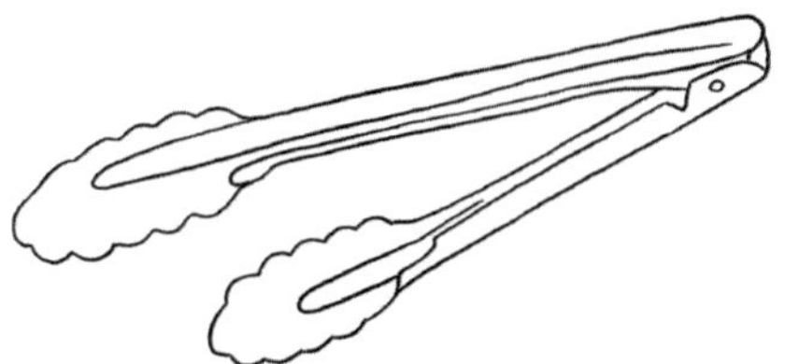

USING POWDERED IRON (FERROUS SULFATE) AS AN AFTERBATH

This is my preferred method for using iron as a modifier because it's easier to control the amount of iron that attaches to the fabric.

1. Dissolve iron at 2% WOF in a nonreactive vessel using warm tap water.

2. Place the dyed textile into the iron solution for one to three minutes, or until it reaches the desired color.

3. Thoroughly rinse the textile in clean water after removing it from the iron solution. The fabric may darken a further one to two shades if it isn't rinsed properly.

WATER TEMPERATURE
Warm or hot water can be used when making an iron solution. The warmer the water, the more rapidly the iron will absorb. It's easier to control the color using cooler water (110–120°F/43–49°C). Keep notes on water temperatures and times so that you can repeat the process with the same results.

USING AN IRON OR COPPER DYE VESSEL OR METAL SCRAPS AS AN AFTERBATH

The biggest advantage to using this method is that the textile absorbs all the extracted metal and there is no residual metal left in the water, which means safe disposal of the water is not required. However, it is a less precise way of creating an afterbath, and you may not be able to repeat results as easily as using powdered metal salts. I prefer this method when using copper.

1. Fill the vessel (or nonreactive pot if using scraps) with water and test the pH. If you use metal scraps, place a wire rack over them for the fabric to sit on; this will protect the fabric from direct contact with the metal pieces.

2. Add small amounts of alum to shift the pH of the water to 4.0. The water needs to be slightly acidic in order to leach out the metal from the vessel or scraps. The amount of alum needed to shift the pH will vary depending on the pot's size and the original pH of the water.

3. Place dyed and pre-wetted fabric into the water and stir to remove air bubbles. Make sure the textile is completely submerged and can move freely. Heat the bath gently until it reaches 195°F (90°C).

4. Remove the fabric once the desired color is reached. Rinse thoroughly.

EQUIPMENT NEEDED

- pH strips
- Alum
- Metal scraps or iron/copper vessel
- Wire rack (if using scraps)

Swatches modified with an iron afterbath.
Left to right: mixed linen dyed with Indian mangrove; mixed linen dyed with Indian mangrove; linen dyed with tara, gallo tannin, and aluminum acetate; linen gauze dyed with tara, gallo tannin, and aluminum acetate; cotton dyed with tara, gallo tannin, and aluminum acetate.

Caring for Naturally Dyed Fabrics

Caring for naturally dyed fabrics takes a little extra time and requires a gentler touch, but it's worth it. To prolong the life of the color and fabric, only wash when needed, either by hand or using the delicate setting on a washing machine, and line dry out of direct sunlight. Avoid direct contact with essential oils or perfume, since they can also affect the color of natural dyes.

LIGHTFASTNESS

All natural dyes will fade over time when exposed to sunlight or any UV light source. Some natural dyes fade very quickly, and others fade gradually over time. Some fade beautifully, and others fade in a way that doesn't resemble the original color. To keep things interesting, dyes high in tannin may darken or become more brown. The best natural dyes, such as madder or cochineal, gently evolve over time, fading slowly and evenly, resulting in a lovely color.

To test for lightfastness, sandwich a fabric sample between two pieces of cardstock or cardboard, leaving a portion of the fabric exposed. Tape or hang this in a window that does not face directly into the sun, and leave it for two to three weeks. After this time, remove the fabric from the window. Add it to your dye journal (see pages 74–77), and record your findings.

Most dyes available for purchase will state how lightfast and washfast they are. It's important to take this into consideration when deciding which dyes to use for particular projects.

RUB-FASTNESS

Proper scouring, mordanting, rinsing, and washing should result in color that does not rub off the surface of textiles. To test for rub-fastness, take a small piece of dry white cloth and, using your fingertip, vigorously rub against the surface of the textile. If color comes off, the textile hasn't been sufficiently rinsed.

WASHFASTNESS

It's important to thoroughly rinse out any excess dye before washing. Good scouring and mordanting will result in dyes that don't wash out. However, some natural dyes are simply not as washfast as others and hand-washing is recommended.

WASHING AND CARE

All naturally dyed textiles should be hand- or machine-washed using a gentle cycle and cool/cold water with a mild pH-neutral detergent, and line dried out of direct sunlight. This will make the color last longer. Do not use commercially produced synthetic fabric softeners since these may shift or effect the longevity of the color. If anything acidic, such as vinegar or citrus juice, is spilled on a textile, run ample cold water over it immediately to dilute/remove it as fast as possible. Strong acids will remove the dye and the mordant, leaving a bleach-like stain if left untreated.

REFRESHING COLOR

When naturally dyed garments or textiles fade, they can always be overdyed. This can be done with the same color/plant or a different one. If a color has faded because of light exposure, you do not need to re-mordant the fabric.

Keep in mind that if the textile has faded unevenly, overdyeing may only lessen the effect. If the textile has faded into an unwanted color, choose a new color that will result in something lovely when layered over the existing color. Remember dye is like watercolor—you can't cover up the base color, you can only transform it.

Troubleshooting

Color shifts, uneven color, and, dull or dingy color are the most common issues that impact dye results. There can be a number of causes behind such issues—below, we explore some of the most common to help you better understand possible problem areas.

UNDERSTANDING WATER

Water can have a huge impact on color depending on the mineral content. The quality of water used when mordanting and dyeing will affect the final results. Soft water is slightly acidic, whereas hard water contains calcium and is usually alkaline. Hard water is great for dyes like madder or weld, but not for cochineal. Acidic water (soft water) can shift colors.

PH strips or a pH meter are readily available to buy online or at local home-improvement stores, these are easy to use to test the pH of your water. Water that is pH neutral is the best for most dyes because it does not alter the color. Modifiers can be added to shift water to the pH best-suited for the particular dye you are using.

If the water contains varying amounts of metal salts, such as iron, it will impact the brightness of color. Yellows will always shift toward chartreuse or olive. The only solution to this is to use filtered or distilled water, or to collect rainwater to use.

My advice is to always test the pH of your water before you get started.

UNEXPECTED DULL COLOR

This is usually the result of overheating, overextracting, or leaving plant matter in the dyebath too long. Most dye materials benefit from a low and slow approach. Of course, there are always exceptions.

UNEVEN DYE RESULTS

Uneven or mottled dyeing can result from improperly scouring fabric, or not thoroughly wetting out fabric before mordanting or dyeing, as well as not rotating fabric evenly or overcrowding fabric during the mordanting or dyeing process.

Streaking is usually the result of not rinsing fabric thoroughly after mordanting/dyeing before drying, and/or the fabric drying too rapidly after mordanting or dyeing.

If you are unhappy with an unevenly dyed piece of fabric, consider using it for experimenting. You could overdye it to test out color combinations.

COLOR CHANGES AFTER WASHING

This can be the result of many things, but water temperature and detergent are usually the culprits. If you are experimenting with foraged plants, some colors are more unstable at certain times of the year. Japanese red maples (*Acer palmatum*) are a good example; they create a striking pink color that shifts to lovely purples when used in the spring and early summer, but only when hand-washed. The rest of the year the leaves create purple-grays, whether hand- or machine-washed.

Safety and Disposal

The general safety guidelines listed below are meant to be helpful, not alarming. Most plant material and additional chemicals we use for natural dyeing are no more harmful than household bleach or cleaning products, many of them less so. However, overexposure and careless handling can result in unpleasant reactions. The best approach is to use common sense.

- Store all dyes, mordants, and assists in clearly labeled containers and keep away from children, pets, and food storage areas.
- Do not eat or drink in the same area while mordanting or dyeing.
- Any equipment used for dye work should never be used for food preparation.
- Put lids on pots or buckets containing mordant, and on dyebaths when unattended.
- Avoid inhaling steam or fumes in the dye process.
- Wearing rubber gloves, an apron/protective clothing, N95 mask or respirator, and protective eyewear while dyeing is recommended.
- Use pot holders when handing hot vessels.
- Always work in a well-ventilated area, preferably outdoors under a covered porch or in a garage.
- Always wear a N95 or respirator when handling fine powders, whether they are toxic or nontoxic—both are potentially hazardous if inhaled.
- Seek medical advice if any substances come into contact with your eyes or mouth.
- Always take extra care when handling any mineral salt mordant. They are irritants and harmful if ingested.

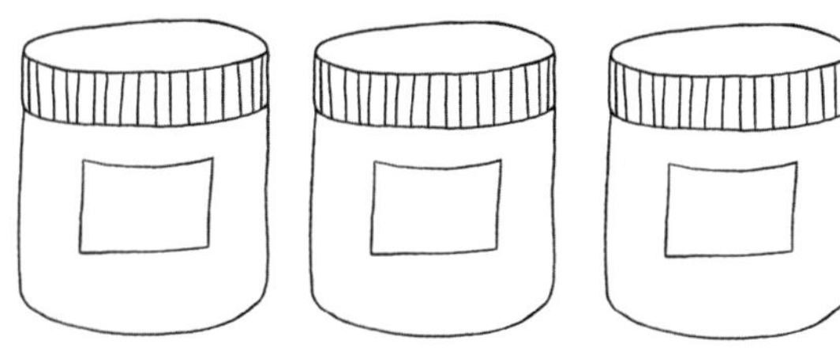

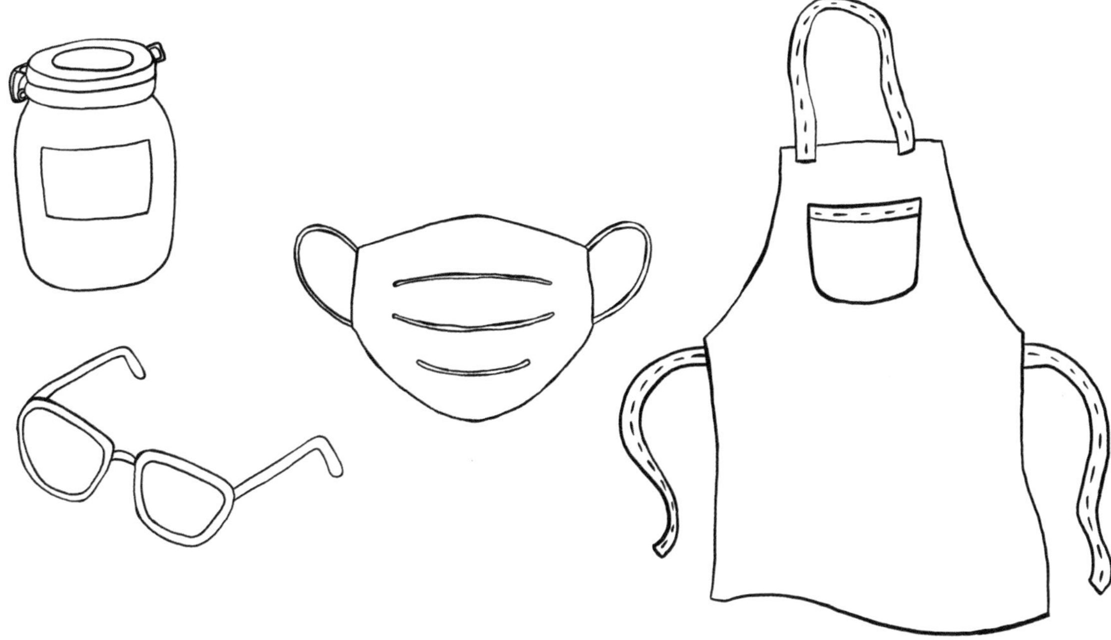

DISPOSAL

You can use exhausted plant matter as mulch or compost it. If this isn't an option for you, place it in a garden waste bin or the garbage.

Dilute mordant or dyebaths and pour onto the garden or use to water plants or grass. You can also pour the diluted solution down the drain. Alkaline or acid afterbaths should be diluted and may be poured down the drain. Pouring the liquid into gravel or dirt driveways is also a good option. In general, try to choose different spots to dispose baths onto. If baths are properly exhausted, there should be hardly any residue remaining. You can always contact your local environmental department if you have any concerns. The retailer you purchased the materials from usually provides safety and disposal guidelines.

SPECIAL CONSIDERATIONS WHEN WORKING WITH IRON

Remember to keep all iron stuff separate and thoroughly clean utensils, vessels, and anything else that comes in contact with iron. Iron is strong and will leave marks even if it has been months since use. I have designated, labeled equipment for iron, including gloves. Use Bar Keepers Friend to clean pots and equipment. Oxalic acid is a primary ingredient and it's specifically formulated to remove rust and mineral deposits, plus it's nontoxic and biodegradable. However, Bar Keepers Friend does not remove rust stains from clothing.

Always wear a mask, gloves, and an apron or protective clothing when handling iron in its powdered form, and gloves and protective clothing when working with an iron bath. There is no way to remove iron from clothing or textiles once it bonds. Wash skin or clothing immediately with soap and cold water if it comes into contact with iron.

Chapter 2
Creating a Color Story

Understanding Color

Making a color wheel is a tried-and-true method for learning about the visual spectrum of color and building your color mixing confidence. The visual color spectrum refers to the seven colors that we see in a rainbow—red, orange, yellow, green, blue, indigo, and violet; think of a color wheel as a circular rainbow, with indigo and violet represented by purple.

Color has its own language and, in order to develop a better understanding, first we need to learn to speak that language. This will help you see the relationships between individual colors in order to use them successfully. All colors are hues, and each hue has three qualities: temperature, saturation, and value.

Temperature refers to how cool or warm a color is. Typically green, blue, and violet are cool hues; while red, orange, and yellow are warm hues. It is important to keep in mind that the temperature can vary significantly within any given color. For example, buttery yellows are warmer, while lemon yellows are cooler.

Saturation is how intense a color appears. A highly saturated color will be vivid and bright, whereas a less saturated color is ethereal or pastel in nature.

Value refers to where a color falls on a black-and-white scale—or how much black or white is mixed into a particular color. In the world of natural dyes we aren't mixing white or black into colors to change the value; adding iron is the closest we get to adding black. I think of mixing natural dyes similarly to mixing watercolors: the colors are transparent, and what the colors are applied to may affect the value.

To get started with color wheels, it is important to understand their foundation: the **primary color triad** of yellow, red, and blue. These colors are located at equal distances around the wheel with yellow at the top. Primary colors can't be mixed from any other combination of colors.

Secondary colors are created by mixing one primary color with another in equal amounts. There are three secondary colors on the color wheel, located at equal distances from each other and the primary colors.

Tertiary colors are created by mixing a primary color with an adjacent secondary color. For example, yellow mixed with orange = yellow-orange. There is a total of six tertiary colors on a twelve-color wheel, each located in between its corresponding primary and secondary colors—these are yellow-orange, red-orange, red-purple, blue-purple, blue-green, and yellow-green.

Making a color wheel

To create a basic color wheel, draw or trace a circle onto a piece of paper with a pencil, then use a ruler to divide the circle into six equal sections. Paint three of the sections with the primary colors yellow, red, and blue, leaving an empty section in between each of the colors. Next, fill the blank spaces with the secondary colors—orange, green, and purple. (Mixing yellow and red creates orange; mixing yellow and blue creates green; and mixing red and blue creates purple). Place orange between red and yellow; green between blue and yellow; and purple between red and blue.

Using watercolors to create your color wheel is a good way to explore color and deepen your understanding of color mixing possibilities without wasting precious natural dyes, especially if you are using expensive dye extracts.

When choosing watercolors, you can buy an "essential" set in small tubes, half pan set, or watercolor sticks. You also have the option of picking colors that resemble the natural dyes you will later be experimenting with. Keep in mind that there is no such thing as a perfect match with watercolors and natural dyes, but here are some good options to start with:

- Rose madder permanent to represent cochineal (*Dactylopius coccus*)
- Permanent red deep to represent madder (*Rubia tinctorium*)
- Imperial purple to represent logwood (*Haematoxylum campechianum*)
- Cadmium yellow to represent weld (*Reseda luteola*)
- Indigo or indanthrone blue to represent indigo (*Indigofera tinctoria*)
- Cascade green to represent chlorophyllin (*Morus alba*)

Going further

If you plan on dyeing fabric or fiber for a specific project, you should also explore complementary and analogous colors. These aren't colors you mix to create other colors, these are the colors you use to make dynamic, moody, and dreamy color stories.

Colors that sit next to each other on the color wheel create a color harmony known as analogous colors. These color hues are very close and create gradient and gentle combinations.

Colors that are directly opposite each other on the color wheel are known as complementary colors. When you place these colors side by side, they create the strongest amount of contrast. Two complementary colors will enhance each other and produce vibrant results.

Once you have made your basic color wheel, try making a color wheel inspired by plant colors. This is a useful way to anticipate the results of mixing natural dyes together. After you have made a couple of plant-inspired color wheels, make a list of each plant that matches the different hues. Then, make a list of natural dyes or plants you can combine to create the hues. Be aware that it is not always possible to replicate the colors on a color wheel exactly using natural dyes.

Unlike watercolors, you might be surprised by the unexpected colors you can create when combining natural dyes. Osage orange and logwood make beautiful chartreuse or olive-green hues when mixed, unlike the brown hues you get when mixing yellow and purple watercolors together—although you can also create brown hues by mixing Osage orange and logwood. Other natural dye plants that produce yellow, such as weld, can be used instead. Keep in mind that resulting hues may vary slightly.

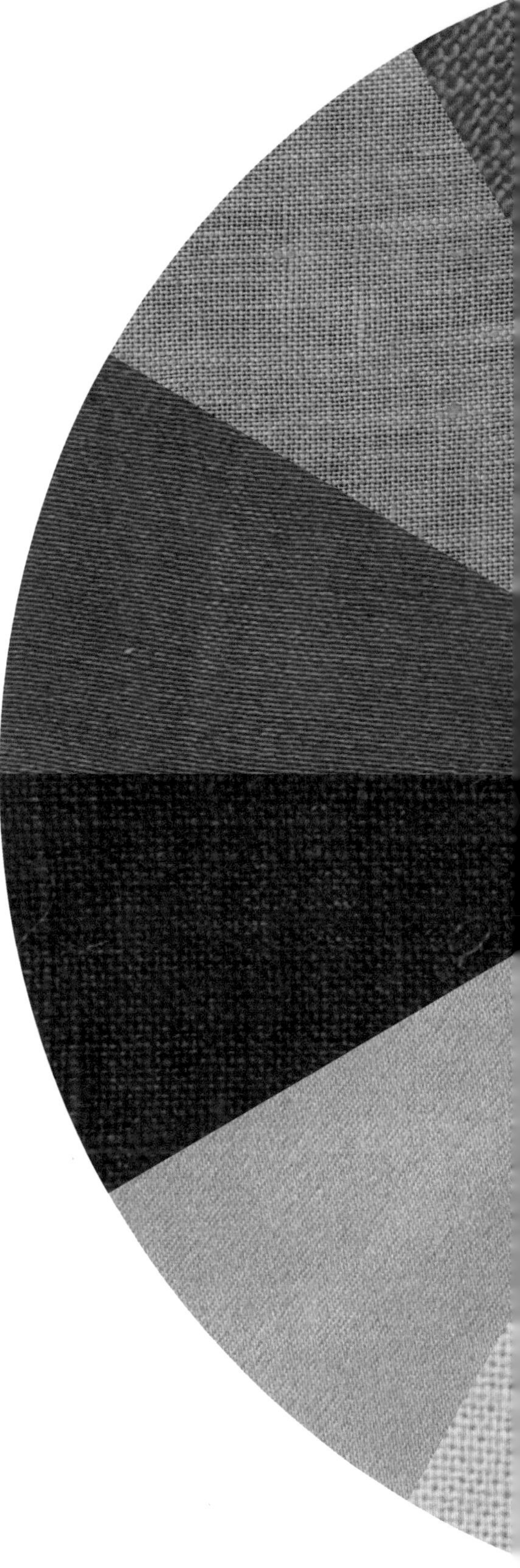

Clockwise from top: madder, munjeet, sulfur cosmos, yellow onion skins, Osage orange, yellow yarrow, St. John's wort, white mulberry, indigo, logwood, lac.

Building Your Color Library

This is my favorite part of the natural dye journey. Nothing is more exciting than exploring new plants and revisiting old favorites. Over the following pages, I guide you through my easy and efficient method for dyeing swatches, which allows you to test many plants simultaneously. During the summer months, when plants are abundant, I test as many as four to eight plants in a week. Enjoy experimenting and building your own color library—you never know what you will get until you try.

Having a bin with fabric swatches organized and ready to go is so helpful when experimenting. Set aside time to get all your fabric/fibers mordanted, cut to size, and color-coded before you begin. I cut 1 x 4-in (2½ x 10-cm) strips and 2 x 2-in (5 x 5-cm) squares. This way you can select what you need and get it soaking while you prep the dye plants and test jars.

I check on my experiments periodically to see if color is developing; if I am happy with the results, I remove the samples and record any important observations in my notebook. If nothing seems to be happening, I let it sit overnight and check it again in the morning. Depending on the plant, it can take as little as two hours, or up to four days, to extract color. The more you experiment, the better you will get at estimating how much time it will take to extract the color you want.

By repeatedly experimenting with the same plants at different times of the growing season I have learned that, in my area, plants produce stronger colors in late summer or early fall. This is because mature leaves usually yield more color than young leaves. For example, horsetail yields more color when picked early in the season and shifts towards beige at the end of its growing season, while stinging nettle creates different colors ranging from yellow, khaki, and olive greens, depending on the time of year. Throughout the seasons I continue to gather and test any plants that show promise and see how far I can push the color.

Living in Northern California, we have experienced extreme weather changes in recent years. Plant colors and harvesting times that had been consistent throughout the drought have shifted with the recent rains. I knew the weather would have an effect, but I didn't fully realize how much of a difference it would make. Plants that I was able to harvest in July and get reliable colors from are now not available until August or September. I can also harvest new plants that are now abundant because of the increase in rain. This dramatic change has made me realize how important it is to record general weather patterns and keep track of what plants I can gather each month.

Small batch dye experiments

EQUIPMENT

Large pot with lid
I recommend a 21-quart (20-liter) enamel canning pot, which will fit five to six jars. They are nonreactive, lightweight, and affordable. Smaller stock pots will work, they just fit fewer jars.

64-oz (1.8-kg) wide-mouth Mason jars or heatproof glass jar with a sealable lid
Make sure there is no rust on the lid, as rust may affect the color results. 32-oz (900-g) jars also work well, but keep in mind that the jar must be large enough to contain plant matter, the dye sample, and enough water for everything to move around freely.

Plant matter
Enough to fill the jar by a third or half way. This may vary depending on the type of plant matter being tested. For example, a single walnut contains a higher pigment ratio than a handful of walnut leaves, and both occupy a very different amount of space in a jar. To start, note approximately how much dye stuff you use in each experiment (eventually, you will intuitively know how much plant matter you need).

Colander or strainer
To remove plant matter, if needed. I use a heatproof plastic colander because metal colanders often rust.

Scissors, pruners, knives, and grinder or pestle and mortar
To process plant matter.

Insulated box or towels/blanket
An energy-efficient way to help maintain temperature.

Heatproof rubber gloves, canning tongs, and hot pads
For handling heated jars and pots safely.

Heat source and power source
Such as an electric hot plate or gas patio burner. When choosing a hot plate, it is crucial to check weight limitations. It is also important to have good ventilation when doing dye work.

Masking tape and permanent marker
To label the tops of jars.

Digital instant-read thermometer
For accurately recording water temperatures.

A wide-mouth funnel
Helpful when adding hot water or transferring dye liquid into another jar.

Bucket or bowl
To create a water bath for soaking fabric swatches.

Hangers, or similar
To hang dye samples on while they dry.

Large cardboard box or a cooler, wool blanket, or cotton towels
You can wrap pots in a variety of textiles to help insulate them as long as the textiles are made from natural fibers. Wool, cotton, and linen work best. Making custom insulation sacks is another great option.

Fabric swatches
Preferably organized and color-coded (see page 67).

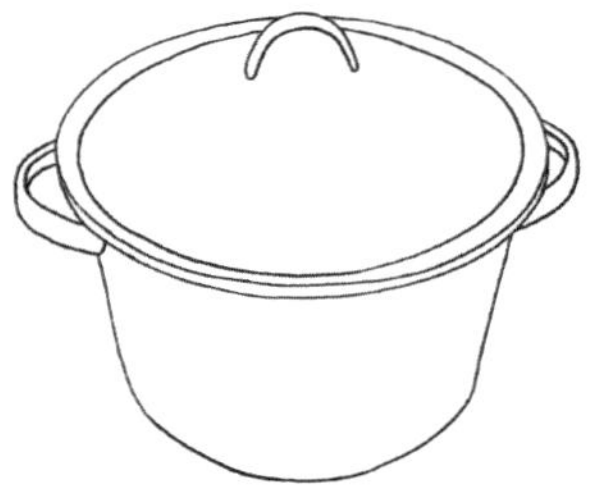

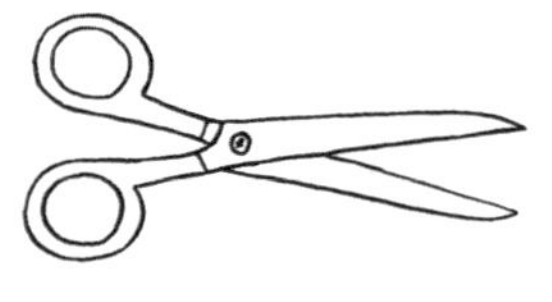

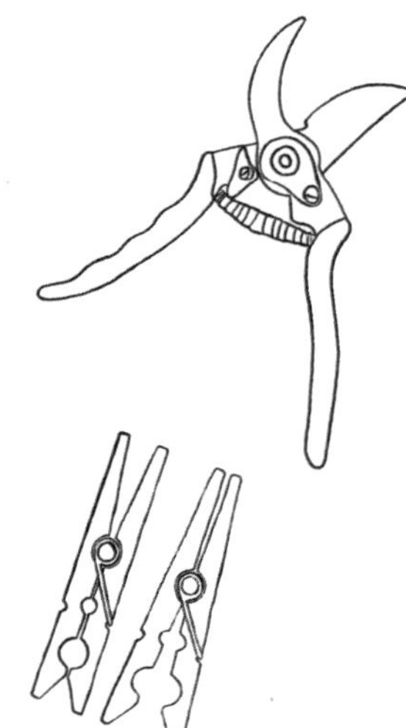

METHOD

The method I use for small batch experiments is a passive way of dyeing. I don't like having to hover over a dyebath, so once it is up to temperature, I am able to turn it off and remove the pot from the heat source, insulate it, and go about my day.

1. Soak your fabric swatches.

2. Process your plants (see pages 37–40 and 42–44), add them to the jars, and label the lids of the jars.

3. Heat enough water to fill the jars and make a water bath to the appropriate temperature. General temperatures are 140–160°F (60–71°C) for flowers, 180°F (82°C) for leaves, and 180–190°F (82–88°C) for roots, bark, acorns, walnuts, seed pods, and pine cones. Once the water is up to temperature, turn off the heat.

4. Add the fabric swatches to the jars and fill with hot water, leaving 1½–2in (3.5–5cm) of room at the top. Gently stir the contents, making sure the swatches are fully submerged, then screw on the lids.

5. Place the jars in the water bath and check the temperature of the water: if it's between 170–180°F (77–82°C), put the lid on the pot, remove it from the heat source, wrap it up, and place it in the insulated box. If the water bath is below 170°F (77°C), reheat it to 180°F (82°C) and then move it to the insulated box.

6. Check the jars in two to four hours to see if any color has developed. If it has, record your findings. If you're happy with the results, remove the fabric swatches and hang them to dry. If color hasn't developed stir the contents, making sure the samples are fully submerged, and slowly reheat.

It can take several days to extract strong color, depending on what plants you are testing. I usually wait until the next morning to check my experiments and record my findings. If I don't see significant color development after four or five days, I'll remove the test swatches, rinse/wash and dry them, and add them to my dye journal along with anything I've learned. If I think boiling and simmering might yield a stronger color, I'll transfer the contents of the jar to a small pot and see what happens after two hours. It is important to remember that it's an experiment, and you learn every time you try a different technique.

MAKING AN INSULATED BOX

There are a couple of ways to insulate a dyebath. For this simple, energy-saving technique, all you need is a cardboard box and/or a reusable insulated bag and towels. Towels should be made with natural fibers, such as cotton, rather than synthetic fibers, which melt.

First, place a towel in the bottom of a cardboard box, then place the covered dyebath containing the jars inside the box on the towel. Drape and wrap a second towel over and around the pot. Close the lid of the box and drape another towel or blanket over the top. This will ensure the box stays closed and further insulates it.

Another great option is to use reusable insulated bags. You must still wrap the dyebath in a towel first since insulated bags are synthetic and will melt if they come into direct contact with a hot pot. Reusable insulated bags can be used in addition to, or instead of, a cardboard box.

Color coding test swatches

Colored locking stitch markers are the most convenient way I have found to keep track of how different fabric swatches were mordanted or treated. These are plastic safety pins generally used for knitting and crochet. I discovered how useful they were when I started teaching natural dye classes: everyone was allocated their own color, plus colors for the different mordants used. We could tell at a glance which sample belonged to who, and it simplified the whole process. If you find it difficult to attach the stitch marker to the fabric, use a darning needle to poke a small hole in the fabric. You can easily attach multiple stitch makers on a fabric swatch. For example, if a swatch has white and turquoise stitch markers, I know at a glance it is gallo tannin combined with aluminum acetate. Once samples are washed and recorded, the stitch markers are removed and ready to use again. Below is the color system I use:

TANNINS

- Gallo tannin–white
- Tara–lilac
- Chestnut–green
- Myrobalan–maroon
- Pomegranate–yellow
- Cutch–orange
- Quebracho–purple
- Fustic–lime green
- Walnut–brown
- Wattle–baby pink

MINERAL SALTS

- Symplocos (plant-based source of aluminum)–red
- Potassium aluminum sulfate–dark blue
- Aluminum acetate–turquoise

MODIFIERS/AFTERBATH

- Iron–black
- Acidic–peach
- Alkaline–mint

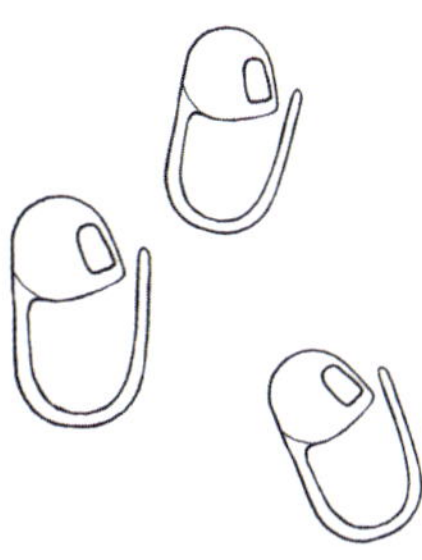

Mixing Colors

When mixing colors, there are a number of different ways to go about the process. You can control the amount of dye by making multiple dyebaths of varying strengths then overdyeing and layering the color, or you can mix colors by combining dyes in the same dyebath.

If you are new to mixing colors, I suggest starting with controlling the amount of dye and learning how the different colors layer. Once you develop a feel for how colors mix, you can progress to combining dyes in a single dyebath. Through a bit of trial and error, and lots of good note taking, you can create your own custom colors and dye recipes.

Using two bold natural dyes, such as cochineal and weld, results in dramatic colors ranging from magentas, fuchsias, and yellows to peaches and oranges. The addition of iron will shift yellow to chartreuse or olive, and magenta to purple. With patience, time, intuition, magick, and a little math, you can easily create over forty color variations from just two natural dyes.

How to mix colors by combining dyes

Layering or overdyeing the previously dyed textile with a secondary color generally results in a more dynamic color. You can use a fresh dyebath or a partly exhausted one. Overdyeing is not recommended for dyes that haven't been mordanted with a mineral salt—the color is not as washfast and will bleed from the fabric and alter the secondary dyebaths.

Mixing two or more dyes in the same dyebath requires more understanding of how colors mix. For example, a strong yellow is dramatically changed when combined with just a small amount of a stronger dye, such as cochineal. When mixing orange, start with yellow, followed by small amounts of pink or red. If you reverse the order and start with a strong amount of pink or red and add a small amount of yellow, there will be almost no perceptible change and this will result in wasting precious dye. I recommend having a bucket of small fabric swatches to test mixed dyebaths. This way, you can test the bath and adjust if necessary.

Creating lighter or softer colors

Most of the time we use natural dyes at their full strength and create different hues by adding fabric at timed intervals and using the exhausted baths to create pale colors. The percentages and method for this is described on page 70. This approach doesn't always result in predictable hues. A partially exhausted bath may give a slightly different color compared to a bath specifically prepared to render a lighter shade. However, depleting a dyebath to create lighter colors is less wasteful. I love overdyeing with a partially exhausted bath—it adds a beautiful nuance to colors.

When more predictable lighter or softer colors are desired, there are two approaches that can be used: smaller percentages of dye can be mixed, yielding lighter hues, or a strong solution can be mixed, measured, and diluted into separate dyebaths. Both methods result in specific hues.

THINGS TO KEEP IN MIND

- Mix colors that are similar in lightfastness. This will ensure that, over time, colors shift and fade at a similar rate, resulting in more harmonious, albeit muted or earthy, versions of the original colors. For example, cochineal and weld have excellent lightfastness, so they are perfect for pairing.
- Using dye extracts at first will give you the most control, resulting in consistent outcomes. However, you can use natural dyes in all forms to mix colors.
- If you choose to modify any of the fabric swatches during the color mixing process, make sure to thoroughly rinse and wash them with pH-neutral soap immediately. This will ensure you won't accidentally contaminate a dyebath if you overdye a modified swatch.

Preparing fabric swatches for overdyeing

The number of swatches you prep depends on how many hues you want to create and the fabrics you are using. I recommend a minimum of three swatches in each base color, in each fabric, excluding natural linen when creating light colors. This will give you a base color swatch and two swatches to overdye and/or modify. If you want to explore overdyeing more swatches, increase the number of fabric swatches to five or seven. You can always save surplus dyed swatches for overdyeing at a later date. It's also good to have a few extra if something doesn't go according to plan.

Creating a custom color code using locking stitch markers is an easy way to organize swatches (see page 67). This allows you to read the stitch marker like a sentence when finished, making it easy to record notes quickly and accurately.

1. Choose the fabrics you want to use. Cut fabric to size—3 x 3in (7.5 x 7.5cm) or 4 x 5in (10 x 12.5cm) are good swatch sizes.

2. Once all the fabric is cut and sorted, attach stitch markers. First, attach the stitch marker color representing the base color: A or B, and sometimes C. Then attach a stitch marker for dark, medium, and light hues.

3. If you're not overdyeing with a second color, add a marker signifying your modifier of choice. If overdyeing with a second color, attach the stitch marker representing this color and a second stitch marker to indicate if it is a dark, medium, or light hue.

4. If using a modifier, add the relevant stitch marker color.

METHOD

1. First, organize your space. Gather your prepared swatches, then label the different soaking buckets, dye pots, and hangers with low-tack masking or flagging tape. Fill the soaking buckets with water and add the fabric swatches so they have plenty of time to soak.

2. Prep the dyebaths by mixing a concentrated solution for colors A, B, and C in separate heatproof jars before transferring them into the dye pots, adding water, and heating them. Save about one-third of the concentrated solutions for colors A and B. Do not mix them together. Set them aside for refreshing or making additional dyebaths for overdyeing. You can also use some of the concentrated solutions to adjust color C, if necessary. The goal is to create dark, medium, and light hues of each color from the three separate dyebaths. You can also make separate dark, medium, and light dyebaths, if preferred.

3. Start with the darkest hues, then work toward lighter hues as the dyebath becomes exhausted. Add fabric swatches at timed intervals, 15–20 minutes apart. Remove dyed swatches when the desired color is achieved. If at any time in the dye process you achieve the desired color in less than 20 minutes, simply remove the fabric, squeeze any excess dye back into the dyebath, and place the fabric in a stop bath (see glossary). This will allow the dye to finish bonding to the fabric.

4. Rinse all swatches before overdyeing with the secondary color—this will prevent the dyebaths becoming contaminated with other colors. Set aside any swatches that you want to keep. I set aside one of each base color, so I can reference what the color looked like before overdyeing.

5. To overdye (if the vats aren't completely exhausted), place the lighter shades of each color into the two other colors, and remove them when the desired color is achieved. If the dyebaths are truly exhausted, replenish them to the desired strength. Starting with the darkest colors and moving to the lightest, place the swatches into the other colors and remove them when the desired color is achieved. For the deepest color, leave the swatch in and remove after all the swatches have been dyed.

6. Rinse the swatches and modify using an afterbath, if desired. Once all the swatches are dyed and/or modified, rinse and wash with pH-neutral soap and hang to dry. I recommend reviewing your fabric samples and notes taken during the process immediately or within three days. Taking time to transfer and organize everything into your dye journal as soon as possible will help you retain what you've learned.

EQUIPMENT NEEDED

- Multiple dye pots: One or two for each color, and one for an optional stop bath
- Pharmaceutical scale for measuring small amounts of extracts and dyestuffs
- Rinsing buckets
- Several small buckets/containers for soaking fabric swatches. I use three for each dye: one for dark, medium, and light.
- Hangers: To keep samples organized during the dye process
- Prepared fabric swatches
- pH paper, if using an acid or alkaline modifier
- Buckets/vessels for modifiers
- Notebook or journal for recording any in-the-moment discoveries
- Low-tack masking tape or flagging tape
- Permanent marker

Cochineal
Weld

Logwood

Osage orange

Cochineal and weld

These are two of my favorite dyes to mix. I used dye extract to create the following colors; if you do not have dye extracts, or if you prefer working with raw dyestuffs, you'll need to adjust the dye percentages.

Dye percentages
Cochineal extract: Light 0.25–0.5% WOF, medium 1–2% WOF, dark 3–4% WOF
Weld extract: Light 0.25–1% WOF, medium 2–3% WOF, dark 4–6% WOF

Dyebaths
Color A: Cochineal
Cochineal extract 10% WOF

Color B: Weld
Weld extract 6% WOF

Color C: Bright tangerine
Cochineal extract 1% WOF, weld extract 3% WOF
Combine the two extracts together to create one dyebath. Note that it will look more pink than orange.

Logwood and Osage orange

Logwood and Osage orange were some of the first natural dyes I used for hand-dyeing garments. On a whim, I took a sun-faded Osage orange dress and overdyed it with logwood and iron. Combining the two dyes resulted in a moody hue that reminded me of shadows in the forest. From that moment on, it became one of my favorite colors. If you do not have dye extracts or prefer working with raw dyestuffs, you'll need to adjust the dye percentages for logwood, since logwood chips don't make as deep of a purple.

Dye percentages
Logwood extract: Light 0.5-1% WOF, medium 2-3% WOF, dark 4-5% WOF
Osage orange sawdust: Light 10-15% WOF, medium 20-30% WOF, dark 50-75% WOF

Afterbath modifiers
White vinegar pH 5
Soda ash pH 9

Dyebaths
Color A: Logwood
Logwood extract 5% WOF

Color B: Osage orange
75% WOF

Color C: Earthy gray purple
Osage orange 30% WOF, logwood 1% WOF
Make two separate solutions, then combine them into one dyebath.

Note: Both logwood and cochineal are pH sensitive. Cochineal shifts towards bright red and pink when the dyebath is acidic and purple when it's alkaline. Logwood shifts towards gray when the dyebath is acidic and purple when it's alkaline on linen and cotton fibers, if the afterbaths are not radically shifted. I like the results I get using white vinegar for an acidic afterbath with a pH 5 and soda ash for an alkaline afterbath with a pH 9.

COCHINEAL AND WELD DYE COMBINATIONS

LOGWOOD AND OSAGE ORANGE DYE COMBINATIONS

Creating a Dye Journal

When building your plant knowledge and color library, it's helpful to create a record of harvested or newly purchased dyes or dye extracts in a dye journal. The time of year, weather, growing conditions, and location can impact the color as much as the fiber, mordant, modifier, and water used when dyeing the fabric swatches. Dye extracts and raw dyestuff often vary in intensity of color. These are just some of the reasons why taking the time to create a dye journal is essential to developing plant and color knowledge and intuition.

The most important thing to keep in mind when making a dye journal is that there is no right or wrong way. You can record as much or as little information as you like. Dye journals can be simple or include drawings, dried plants, ideas for color stories, musings, projects, maps, and photos. Think about keeping multiple journals. One journal might be for recording dye swatches and your process, including what you did, when you did it, and what you expected compared to the true outcome. Other journal ideas include a collection of plant sketches, ideas, and inspiration, and a journal focusing on just one plant or all the plants that give you a specific color. Wouldn't it be wonderful to have a book of sunshine filled with pages of yellow rainbows? Once you hone your dye recipes and process, I recommend making separate recipe cards and/or a recipe book.

My main dye journal is a simple A5 notebook with blank pages that I have filled with experiments, to-do lists, mistakes, and post-it notes. It's a mess, but it's part of my process and what works for me. I take all the useful information from that journal and transcribe it into an organized ring binder.

Getting started

Some things are essential to keep track of if you want to recreate colors and grow your plant knowledge. If it's not written down, you won't remember. You can still lose yourself in the process, just scribble some notes down and take some pictures as you go.

TOOLS AND MATERIALS

Note/sketchbook or ring binder and paper

I have around seven dye journals that I've started, abandoned, and started again. It took me a while to find a note/sketchbook that fit my needs. Size, page count, type of page, and the feel of the paper can make a difference. My favorite journal is a slim A5 or traveler's notebook with sketch or watercolor paper. I found that journals with higher page counts became too bulky once fabric swatches were added. Japanese ring binders, which can have as many as thirty rings to accommodate all the different sizes of Japanese loose-leaf paper, are another favorite of mine. They allow more freedom and the ability to add, remove, or rearrange pages. Best of all, you can remove any important pages from abandoned dye journals and add them to a ring binder.

Writing implements

I use a pencil or erasable pen for numbering pages and writing in the index so that I can change page numbers and adjust my index if I add or remove anything.

Glue for attaching swatches

I use PH-neutral PVA paper bookbinding glue and a small paintbrush. I have not found a PH-neutral gluestick. If you use something that's not PH-neutral, it may affect the color of your swatch.

Other useful items

Highlighters, colored pencils, watercolors, tape, paperclips, a stapler, a hole punch, a cutting mat or cardboard, and a ruler are also useful when creating your dye journals.

ATTACHING SWATCHES TO YOUR DYE JOURNAL

I use a few different methods for attaching swatches/fibers neatly to a page. First I gather all my notes, samples, and anything else I need, and make sure my workspace is organized.

If I'm attaching fabric swatches, I make sure they are ironed and flat. With a ruler and pencil, I draw light lines where I'll attach the swatches. Next I apply a very thin layer of PVA glue to the paper. I lay the swatch on top of the line and gently pat the fabric. PVA glue is very thick and generally doesn't bleed through the fabric unless you apply too much glue or press down on the fabric really hard. When attaching very thin fabric, use as little glue as possible.

For yarn, roving, or ribbon, there are a couple of different options:

Option 1: Using a hole punch, make a series of evenly spaced holes approximately ½in (12mm) or more from the edge of the paper. Loop and secure the sample through the hole. If you're using a journal and not a ring binder, secure the cardstock in the journal with tape, glue, staples, or paper clips.

Option 2: Using an exacto knife make slits in the paper or cardstock and weave samples through the paper. You can place a piece of cardboard underneath the paper to protect the other pages or work surface.

KEY INFORMATION TO INCLUDE

It is ultimately entirely up to you what information you would like to keep in your dye journal. Some suggestions can be found below, but you can adjust these to suit your needs:

- Date
- Weather conditions, if using foraged plants
- Contents of fabric
- Special equipment—any tools used or tools you wish you had
- Weight of fiber (WOF)
- Mordants
- Modifiers or afterbath—record the length of time in the afterbath. Did you use a nonreactive pot?
- Dye material and how it was processed
- Temperature and length of time fabric spent in the dye bath
- PH of the water, if applicable
- Did anything unexpected happen?
- How the fabric was washed after dyeing—hand washing vs machine washing may affect color results
- Optional: a picture or illustration of the plant

ORGANIZING YOUR DYE JOURNAL

It can be challenging and overwhelming to keep track of the different fibers, mordants, and modifiers—creating a system makes it easy. Recording information can take a considerable amount of time, and over the years I've learned the most important part is to simplify as much as possible. Create a system that makes sense to you, be consistent, and develop good habits. Here are some organizational tips for your dye journal:

- Reserve the first three pages of your journal for an index or table of contents. Number the pages as you go and record the dye plant/experiment and the page number in the index.
- Include samples of undyed fabrics and fibers. Always attach your samples in the same order. By arranging the dyed samples in the same order as the undyed samples, you know what fabrics/fibers you used.
- Using abbreviations and symbols is a great way to save time. Create your own in a way that works for you; just be sure to create a key at the beginning of your journal, to refer back to.

Types of dye journal

BASIC DYE JOURNAL

This journal is full of practical information. A reference guide where you record everything you learned from your experiments. A place to transcribe your notes and any loose pieces of paper along with the dye sample and the key information from the checklist.

A COLOR RECIPE BOOK

Having a separate color recipe book is convenient and key to easily replicating colors. I have one recipe book for commercial extracts and raw dyestuffs and one for plants I forage or grow. I use a small B7 ring binder. It holds paper about the size of an index card. Each color has its own card with a fabric swatch, extract, or raw dyestuff used, where the dyestuff was purchased, foraged, or grown, and all the basic information needed to replicate that color.

I don't make recipe cards for all the plants I forage, just those that produce exceptional color and have specific processes. Loquat trees are one of those super magical plants that I can get seven-plus shades of pinks, mauves, peaches, and oranges from, depending on how the plant is processed and the time of year it's harvested. It took me a summer of experimenting before I remembered that to get certain pinks tones I needed to steep the leaves for a specific amount of time and discard that liquid, then add fresh water and continue. This was a key piece of information that I simply forgot to write down. I would've saved so much time and frustration if I had stopped for a moment and taken notes.

ADVENTURES, MUSINGS, AND PLANT MAGIC NOTEBOOK

This is where I dream about colors, plants, and projects. I write about the feeling I get when finding a new plant. The experience of gathering, processing, and watching the color appear. I still remember the day I found a tiny patch of native mugwort. We had no mugwort on the property for 12 years and then suddenly it was there, like the plant knew I needed it. I patiently waited and tended the plants for two years before the mugwort patch was thriving and abundant enough that I could harvest and use it for dye.

This journal is a place to put your plant samples, observations, places and plants you want to explore, and projects using what you've learned. If you use herbs or edible plants or flowers, consider adding a recipe for tea, herbal tincture, or food you can make using a particular plant. Think about including historical uses or plant lore to deepen your relationship with specific plants.

SEASONAL COLOR FOLK METHOD FIELD GUIDE

This dye journal can be seasonal or monthly, and provide a deep dive into exploring the secret colors hiding within the landscape and plants you walk by daily. Include dye recipes that have basic guidelines for creating colors, and a list of plants organized by color that are available each month. Many plants have a short harvest time. Field horsetail, for example, has a reproductive stem before it fronds which contains spores that are rich in pigment and can be selectively harvested as long as they are abundant. This aspect of the plant is only available for a short window of time. The fronds have a longer harvest season and yield the same color, but you need a larger quantity. Creating a field guide is a great way to expand your understanding of the magickal qualities of plants.

Chapter 3
Color Library

A Library of Natural Colors

This library will take you through a whole rainbow of natural dyes and includes commercially produced dyes that are readily available and easy to source online; flowers, leaves, seeds, nuts, and fungi that can be foraged; as well as plants that can be grown in a home garden. To expand the color range even further, try using a variety of fabrics—linen, wool, cotton, and silk all take dye differently. Substantive natural dyes (marked with an "S") can bond to fabric without a mordant, while adjective dyes ("A") require one. Mordants, where used, are listed in brackets next to the material of the swatch pictured. Gallo tannin ("GT"), aluminum acetate ("AA"), and aluminum triformate ("AT") have been used. The WOF percentages required for dyebaths are also listed.

Pinks, reds, and purples

A

COCHINEAL (*DACTYLOPIUS COCCUS*)

Cochineal is a scale insect native to subtropical South America through the southwest United States, that lives on prickly pear (nopal) cacti. Cochineal (fertile females) and their host cacti are cultivated together on farms called nopalries. They are hand-harvested after about ninety days. This labor-intensive process is one of the reasons why cochineal is so expensive and very precious. Just small amounts of cochineal produce a striking range of fuchsias, reds, and purples.

Left to right: mixed linen (GT & AA), white linen (GT & AA), cotton (GT & AA), linen gauze (GT & AA), white linen (GT & AA), silk (AT), white linen (GT & AA).
Ground insect: medium 3–8%, dark 10% WOF. **Extract**: light 0.25–0.5%, medium 1–2%, dark 3–4% WOF.

S

COASTAL REDWOOD CONES (*SEQUOIA SEMPERVIRENS*)

Coastal redwoods have tiny, green, jewel-like cones. Begin looking for them in late July and throughout the fall. Fresh green or partly dried cones yield rich plummy colors, mauves, and soft pinks. As the cones age and dry out, the colors become more earthy. It's important to collect cones before the rainy season washes the pigment away. When mordanted with aluminum salts, the color shifts toward a dull gray earthy purple.

Top to bottom: white linen, silk, cotton, linen gauze, white linen (GT & AA), cotton (GT & AA), linen gauze (GT & AA). **Cone:** medium 50%, dark 100% WOF.

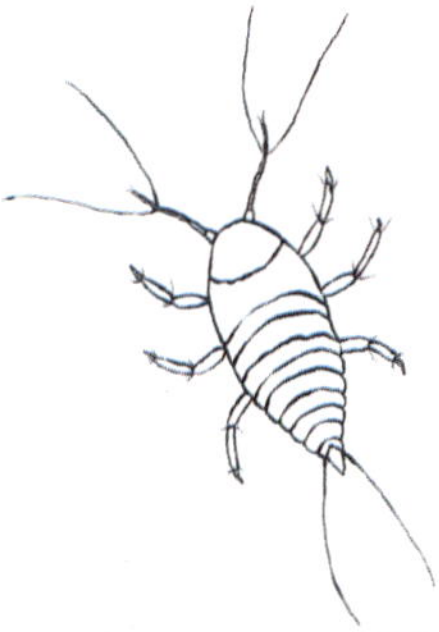

A

LAC (*LACCIFER LACCA*)

Lac is an ancient dye from the secretions of the female lac bug found throughout India, southeast Asia, Nepal, and China. The colorant used for natural dyeing is extracted from the harvested resin (stick lac), the raw material for shellac. Lac extract is an affordable alternative to cochineal (see page 80) and yields similar colors but softer and warmer shades. Premium lac extract yields bright raspberry and fuchsia.

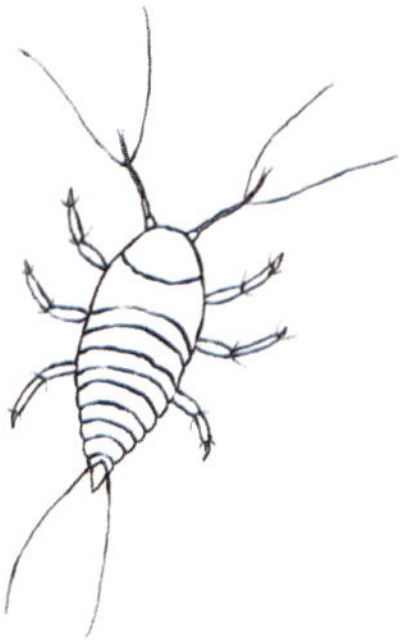

Left to right: linen gauze (GT & AA), silk (AT), white linen (GT & AA), white linen (GT & AA), mixed linen (GT & AA), white linen (GT & AA), cotton (GT & AA).
Extract: light 1–3%, medium 4–6%, dark 7–12% WOF.

A

NUTSEDGE (*CYPERUS ERAGROSTIS*)

Also known as tall flatsedge, nutsedge is one of those plants that completely surprised me. It yields beautiful soft pinks similar to horsetail. Generally found in wetlands, nutsedge is native to the western United States, but has become naturalized across North America, Europe, and parts of South America and Australia, where it's considered an invasive weed.

Left to right: silk (AT), white linen (GT & AA), white linen (GT & AA), linen gauze (GT & AA), wool (AT).
Flowering tops: 100% WOF.

S

FIELD HORSETAIL (*EQUISETUM ARVENSE*)

Also known as foxtail-rush, horsetail belongs to one of the oldest living plant families in the world, dating back to the Carboniferous period. The cone-topped fertile stems appear in early spring. Sterile frilly shoots grow during the summer months. Both variations produce soft pinks on unmordanted cellulose fibers, and dusty mauves on unmordanted protein fibers or cellulose fibers mordanted with aluminum salts. Only use fertile stems if there is an abundance of plants. If cultivating field horsetail in a garden, it will need regular management to keep it in check.

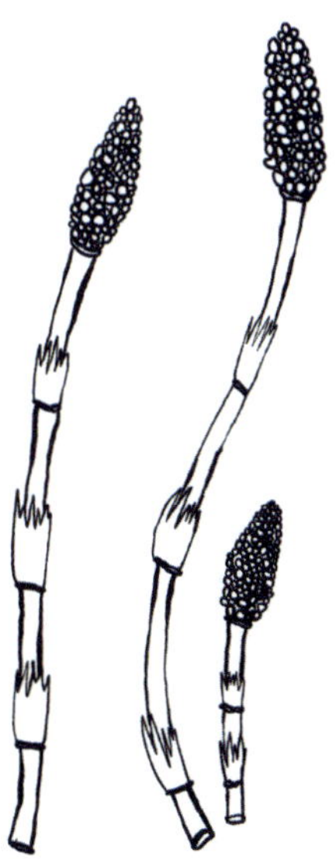

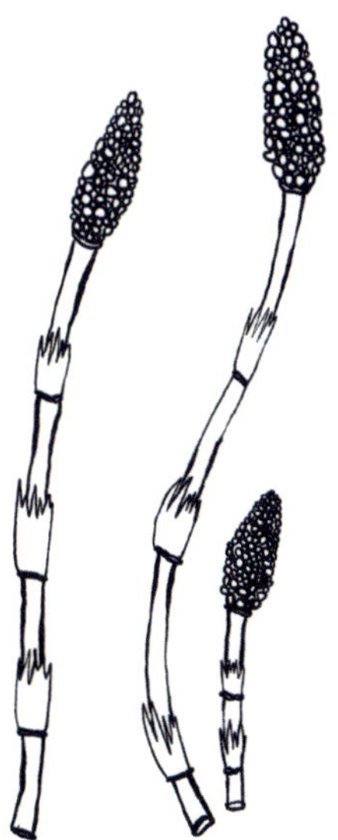

Top to bottom: white linen, mixed linen (GT & AA), cotton, linen (GT & AA), white linen, wool, linen (GT & AA).
Plant: 100% WOF.

A

MUNJEET (*RUBIA CORDIFOLIA*)

Munjeet (also known as Indian madder) is one of European madder's close relatives (see page 87), and the two plants have been used to create reds on textiles for centuries. Unlike *Rubia tinctorum*, *Rubia cordifolia* is not as affected by high temperature and is more orange-red in color on both cellulose and protein fibers. Munjeet is grown in India; it is a prized herb in Ayurveda and is available as ground root for dyeing.

Top to bottom: linen gauze (GT & AA), mixed linen (GT & AA), cotton (GT & AA), silk (AT), cotton (GT & AA), white linen (GT & AA), white linen (GT & AA).
Ground root: medium 50%, dark 100% WOF.

S

MANZANITA (*ARCTOSTAPHYLOS* SPP.)

Manzanita is easy to spot by its twisted branches and smooth mahogany bark that's often cool to the touch, even in warm weather. Over 40 native species are found in western North America. The bark naturally sheds around the summer solstice and is easy to gather at this time of year and into the fall. Depending on the species, the bark creates beautiful colors ranging from blushing pinks to earthy mauves and red-browns. The leaves produce soft yellows and golden ochers with an aluminum salt mordant.

Left to right: white linen (GT & AA), silk (AT), wool, cotton (GT & AA), wool (AT), mixed linen (GT & AA), linen gauze. **Bark**: 50–100% WOF.

A

DYER'S ALKANET (*ALKANNA TINCTORIA*)

Dyer's alkanet is a herbaceous flowering plant in the borage family, also known as dyer's bugloss or Spanish bugloss. The pigment is extracted from the roots of the plant and used in cosmetics, soaps, and pigments. Alkanet is not water-soluble and must be soaked in a solution of rubbing alcohol and hot water before a dyebath is made. Colors on mordanted fabric range from shades of gray to lavender and purple.

Left to right: white linen (GT & AA), linen gauze (GT & AA), cotton (GT & AA), mixed linen (GT & AA), silk (AT), wool (AT), white linen (GT & AA).
Ground root: medium 50–75%, dark 100% WOF.

S

BLACK CUTCH (*SENEGALIA CATECHU*)

Cutch is a brown dye that has been used in India since ancient times. The extract is derived from the heartwood and pods of black cutch trees. Cutch is sweet-smelling and very easy to use. Colors can range from rich red-browns to golden yellow-browns or lovely chocolate browns. Cutch is high in tannins, making it an excellent dye for cellulose fibers. The addition of 2% WOF soda ash to the dyebath will shift the hue towards red and dramatically deepen the color.

Left to right: linen (GT & AA), cotton, silk (AT), linen gauze, mixed linen (GT & AA), cotton (GT & AA), linen gauze (GT & AA).
Extract: light 2–5%, medium 7–15%, dark 20–30% WOF.

S

LOGWOOD (*HAEMATOXYLUM CAMPECHIANUM*)

Logwood has been prized as a natural dye since the sixteenth century. Before synthetic dyes, nearly all black cloth was dyed with a combination of logwood and iron, a difficult color to achieve with natural dyes. Logwood by itself is not very lightfast. A pinch of iron will deepen the color and dramatically improve the lightfastness. Mix it with weld (see page 112) and you'll make green!

Left to right: mixed linen (GT & AA), white linen (GT & AA), silk (GT & AA), wool (GT & AA), linen gauze (GT & AA), white linen (GT & AA), white linen.
Wood chips: medium 10–15%, dark 20–39% WOF. **Extract:** light 0.5–1%, medium 2–3%, dark 4–5% WOF.

A

MADDER (*RUBIA TINCTORUM*)

Madder has been used for centuries and is one of the oldest known natural dyes. It can be cultivated in gardens; the plants should be grown for at least three to four years before harvesting the roots for dyeing. Madder can be purchased as an extract, ground, or whole root, with each form having its own unique characteristics.

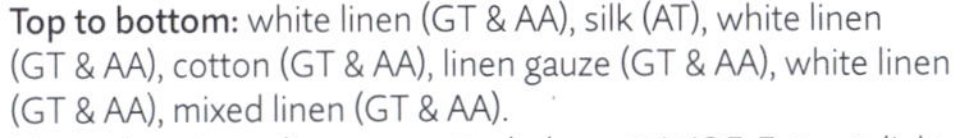

Top to bottom: white linen (GT & AA), silk (AT), white linen (GT & AA), cotton (GT & AA), linen gauze (GT & AA), white linen (GT & AA), mixed linen (GT & AA).
Ground root: medium 20–30%, dark 100% WOF. **Extract:** light 1–2%, medium 3%, dark 4–10% WOF.

S

QUEBRACHO (MORENO EXTRACT) (*SCHINOPSIS QUEBRACHO-COLORADO*)

Quebracho is an evergreen tree that grows wild in South America. The name comes from two Spanish words, *quebrar* and *hacha*, meaning "ax breaker," due to the hardness of the wood. Quebracho is high in tannin and ideal for use on cellulose fibers. It can be used as a mordant or a dye. Depending on the mordant and fiber content, the colors vary from earthy peach to coral and yellow.

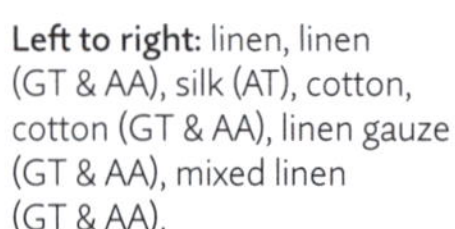

Left to right: linen, linen (GT & AA), silk (AT), cotton, cotton (GT & AA), linen gauze (GT & AA), mixed linen (GT & AA).
Extract: light 1–2%, medium 3–6%, dark 10–15% WOF.

S

BLACK WATTLE (*ACACIA MEARNSII*)

Wattle extract comes from the wood of black wattle acacia trees. It has a high tannin content and is used both for natural dyeing and tanning leather. Wattle is a catechin or red-brown tannin like quebracho and cutch (see above and page 86). It will impart a light pinky-beige color and has a toasty wood smell. Natural dyers use wattle extract to create soft pinks, peachy tans, and iron-based grays and blacks.

Left to right: cotton (GT & AA), linen (GT & AA), cotton, linen, silk (AT), linen gauze (GT & AA), mixed linen (GT & AA).
Extract: light 1–3%, medium 5%, dark 7–10% WOF.

S

SILVER WATTLE (*ACACIA DEALBATA*)

Silver wattle is native to Australia and considered an invasive species in California. It's found in the coastal ranges, San Francisco Bay area, and south coast of California. I like experimenting with invasive plants and was delighted by the colors made from the seed pods. Ripe seed pods can be gathered once they turn purply brown, usually mid-July into the fall. They make the most beautiful earthy purples and browns depending on the mordant used, while the leaves make vibrant yellows to olive greens.

Top to bottom: cotton (GT & AA), mixed linen (GT & AA), silk (AT), linen gauze, wool, white linen (GT & AA), white linen (GT & AA, with the leaves as the dyestuff).
Pods: 100% WOF. **Leaves:** 100–300% WOF.

Top to bottom: cotton (GT & AA), white linen (GT & AA), linen gauze (GT & AA), silk (AT), mixed linen (GT & AA), white linen (GT & AA), white linen (GT & AA).
Ground root: medium 50–100%, dark 200% WOF.

A

PURPLE GROMWELL (*LITHOSPERMUM ERYTHRORHIZON*)

The root of purple gromwell is called shikon (purple root) in Japan and is an ancient dye dating from Nara period (710–794 CE). This delicate purple color was reserved exclusively for the highest ranks of Japanese society and forbidden for commoners to wear. The plant is part of the borage family and is similar to dyer's alkanet (see page 85).

S

SAPPANWOOD (CAESALPINIA SAPPAN)

Also known as eastern Brazilwood, sappanwood is native to southeast Asia and India and is used to make a traditional Japanese dye called suoh. Depending on the pH level of your dyebath, startling color variations range from deep reds to purples and even oranges. The fine, sawdust-like natural dye powder of sappanwood is renewable and sustainable and is one of the "exotic" redwood dyes. This wood is high in tannin but is only lightfast when mordanted.

Left to right: silk (AT), linen gauze (GT & AA), mixed linen (GT & AA), white linen (GT & AA), cotton (GT & AA). **Sawdust**: medium 20–30%, dark 50–100% WOF.

Yellows, Golds, Peaches, and Oranges

A

APPLE (*MALUS DOMESTICA*)

Apple trees are widely available and easy to grow. Their leaves yield soft, vivid, and deep-golden yellows. Older leaves yield the strongest color and should be harvested in the summer months and into the fall before the leaves change color. I use Gravenstein apple leaves (*Malus gravenstein*), a specific variety that has been part of the Sonoma County landscape for more than 200 years. I love overdyeing apple leaves with cochineal to make tangerine colors.

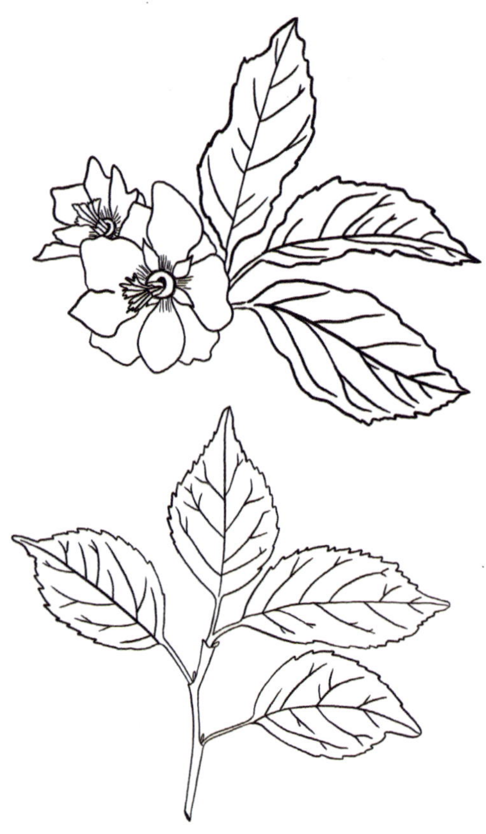

Top to bottom: cotton (GT & AA), mixed linen (GT & AA), silk (AT), white linen (GT & AA), white linen (GT & AA), white linen (GT & AA).
Leaves: 100–300% WOF.

A

AFRICAN MARIGOLD (*TAGETES ERECTA*)

African marigolds (Aztec marigolds) are a potent natural dye and produce more dye than French marigolds (see page 96). They bloom from late summer through the first frost. The more flowers you harvest, the more blooms the plant produces. Colors range from soft yellows to deep golds to olive greens, depending on the mordant or modifier used. The flowers can be used fresh or dried. Dried flowers and marigold extract can be purchased online.

Left to right: silk (AT), white linen (GT & AA), linen gauze (GT & AA), white linen (GT & AA), mixed linen (GT & AA).
Flowers: 75–100% WOF.

A

AMUR SILVER GRASS (*MISCANTHUS SACCHARIFLORUS*)

Kariyasu is a traditional natural dye in Japan. The dried leaves have been used as a yellow dye since ancient times. In the Nara period (710–794 CE), Kariyasu was used to dye cloth for common people's clothes. Amur silver grass is now widely cultivated as an ornamental grass in temperate climates around the world.

Left to right: silk (AT), linen gauze (GT & AA), white linen (GT & AA), white linen (GT & AA), cotton (GT & AA), mixed linen (GT & AA).
Dried grass: 100% WOF.

S

ROCK BUCKTHORN BERRY (*RHAMNUS SAXATILIS*)

Rock buckthorn berries (Avignon berry) were used for making green ink in medieval times and have been used as a natural dye for hundreds of years. They make a strong, warm, lightfast yellow to yellow-green dye that combines well with other dyes. Depending on fiber, mordant or modifier, and pH levels, slightly different tones can be achieved, adding to the allure of this natural dye. To make almost black, try overdyeing with a combination of logwood extract and iron.

Left to right: silk (AT), linen gauze (GT & AA), white linen (GT & AA), mixed linen (GT & AA), white linen (GT & AA), cotton (GT & AA). **Extract:** light 1–2%, medium 5%, dark 10% WOF.

S

COAST LIVE OAK (*QUERCUS AGRIFOLIA*)

The coast live oak is an iconic, majestic tree that can live for centuries. They are easily recognized by their gnarled branches; small, spiky leaves; and grand canopy. The coast live oak loves the fog and mild winters. Its acorns are the last to ripen in the fall, and over 270 species of bird and butterfly rely on these trees for habitat and food.

Left to right: cotton (GT & AA), linen, linen gauze (GT & AA), linen (GT & AA), silk (AT). **Leaves:** 100–200% WOF.

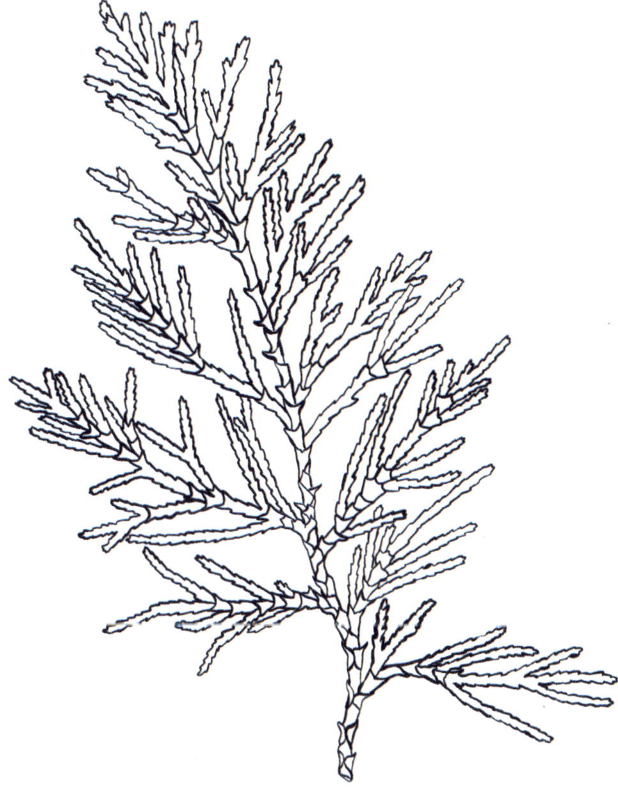

A

INCENSE CEDAR (*CALOCEDRUS DECURRENS*)

Cedar is an evergreen coniferous tree, widely cultivated as an ornamental plant. Known as the tree of life, it's said to house nature deities and spirits of ancestors, and brings protection to those who ask permission before gathering foliage. It yields soft yellow, bright lemon yellows, and green, depending on the mordant and modifier used.

Top to bottom: silk (AT), white linen (GT & AA), linen gauze (GT & AA), white linen, white linen (GT & AA), cotton (GT & AA).
Foliage: 100–300% WOF.

A

DYER'S CHAMOMILE (*ANTHEMIS TINCTORIA*)

Dyer's chamomile (golden marguerite) is an extremely productive, low-maintenance perennial dye plant. Dried or fresh flowers produce a beautiful, sweetly fragrant, warm yellow dye that is more lightfast than many other yellow dyes. If the first flowers are harvested promptly, plants may produce another flush. As a bonus, it attracts beneficial insects like soldier beetles and syrphid flies.

Left to right: silk (AT), mixed linen (GT & AA), linen gauze (GT & AA), white linen (GT & AA), white linen (GT & AA). **Dried flower**: medium 75%, dark 100–200% WOF.

A

FRENCH MARIGOLD (*TAGETES PATULA*)

French marigolds, despite their name, are native to Mexico, and have a wide range of fiery colors. They are popular garden plants, easy to grow in pots, and are found almost everywhere. Marigolds are prolific bloomers and can be used fresh or dried. Different times of year and different varieties yield colors ranging from yellow and orange to tan and even olive green.

Left to right: linen gauze (GT & AA), white linen (GT & AA), white linen (GT & AA), mixed linen (GT & AA), cotton (GT & AA), silk (AT), wool (AT). **Dried flower**: 75–100% WOF.

S

DOUGLAS-FIR (*PSEUDOTSUGA MENZIESII*)

Douglas fir is native to western North America. Despite its common name, it is not a true fir, spruce, or pine. It is also not a hemlock; the genus name *Pseudotsuga* means "false hemlock." Douglas fir is a wonderful tree to explore. Depending on the part of the tree used and the addition of a mordant, colors can range from peaches, soft tans, and yellows to chartreuse. You can create an entire color story with one tree.

Cone, left to right: cotton, linen gauze, silk (AT), wool (AT), mixed linen (GT & AA), white linen (GT & AA), white linen.
Cone: 100–200% WOF.

Bark, left to right: white linen (GT & AA), linen gauze, wool (AT), silk, white linen, mixed linen (GT & AA), cotton (GT & AA).
Inner bark: 100% WOF.

First extraction, left to right: mixed linen (GT & AA), linen (GT & AA), silk (AT), linen (GT), cotton (GT & AA), wool (AT).
Dried petals: 100–200% WOF.

Second extraction, left to right: cotton, linen gauze, linen, silk.

A

SAFFLOWER (*CARTHAMUS TINCTORIUS*)

Safflower, a thistle-like plant with yellow flowers, is one of the oldest known dyestuffs. Depending on the method and fiber used, safflower produces vibrant yellow and pink colors, orange/coral tones, and even reds. However, wool and other protein fibers (except silk) will not take the pink colorant. Safflower is a stunning addition to any home garden.

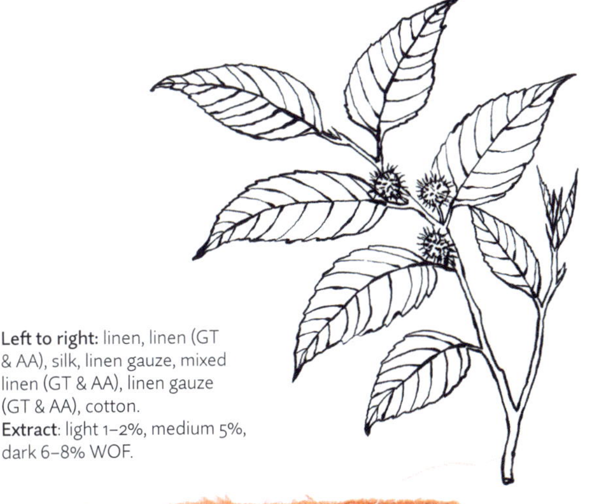

S

OLD FUSTIC (*MACLURA TINCTORIA*)

Old fustic comes from a tall, tropical hardwood tree that grows from Mexico to Argentina. It's high in tannic acid, which makes it ideal for dyeing cellulose fibers. It has a high light- and washfastness, and exposure to strong sunlight may actually darken colors. Fustic produces colors ranging from peaches to daffodil yellow and deep golds. Try overdyeing fustic with madder or cochineal to make oranges, and with logwood or iron for olive greens.

Left to right: linen, linen (GT & AA), silk, linen gauze, mixed linen (GT & AA), linen gauze (GT & AA), cotton.
Extract: light 1–2%, medium 5%, dark 6–8% WOF.

S

POMEGRANATE (*PUNICA GRANATUM*

Pomegranate dye is made from the leathery skins of pomegranate fruit. The peels are high in tannin and are used as both a dye and a mordant. Pomegranate yields a green-yellow color that shifts to olive and dark gray with iron. The skins can be purchased as dried peels, ground powder, or as an extract. In plant lore, pomegranate is used for wishing magick, so remember to make a wish before making a dyebath.

Left to right: silk (AT), cotton, linen gauze, white linen, white linen (GT & AA), linen gauze (GT & AA), mixed linen (GT & AA).
Dried rind: 20% WOF.
Extract: light 1–3%, medium 5%, dark 7–10% WOF.

A

DYER'S COREOPSIS (*COREOPSIS TINCTORIA*)

Coreopsis, also known as tickseed, has over seventy species growing wild, mostly in North America. It's perfect for growing in the garden. Coreopsis produces prolific amounts of flowers if picked daily and can be used fresh or dried. Colors range from deep oranges and golden yellows to rust browns and corals. For reddish shades, shift the pH of the dyebath with a pinch of soda ash and watch it magically turn redder! Dried flowers can be purchased online.

Top to bottom: mixed linen (GT & AA), silk (AT), linen gauze (GT & AA), white linen (GT & AA), white linen (GT & AA).
Dried flowers: 100% WOF.

A

AMUR CORK (*PHELLODENDRON AMURENSE*)

Kihada is a traditional yellow dye from the Amur cork tree that grows wild in the mountains of Japan. The inner bark produces a yellow dye that has been used since ancient times on fabric and Japanese paper because of its insect-repellent properties. It's also one of the fifty fundamental herbs used in traditional Chinese medicine.

Left to right: linen gauze (GT & AA), silk (AT), cotton (GT & AA), mixed linen (GT & AA), white linen (GT & AA). **Inner bark:** 100% WOF.

S

HAWTHORN (*CRATAEGUS MONOGYNA*)

Hawthorn, also known as quickthorn, is a tree with white or pink flowers and edible berries. The leaves produce a beautiful range of oranges. The strongest colors come from leaves gathered in late summer or early fall, especially if those leaves are left in the dyebath for a couple of days and then strained out.

Left to right: silk, linen gauze, linen gauze (GT & AA), white linen, mixed linen (GT & AA), wool, cotton (GT & AA). **Leaves:** 100% WOF.

A

KUCHINASHI (*GARDENIA JASMINOIDES*)

Kuchinashi is the most popular gardenia species, prized for its seed pods and fragrant white flowers that bloom in spring and summer. It can be cultivated in gardens as an ornamental plant. Gardenia seeds are a traditional Japanese natural dye for fabric and tinting foods. The seed pods look like a bunch of little birds opening their beaks, which is fitting, considering they create a rich, vibrant yellow that sings.

Left to right: white linen (GT & AA), mixed linen (GT & AA), linen gauze (GT & AA), cotton (GT & AA), silk (AT), white linen (GT & AA).
Dried seeds: 50–100% WOF.

A

JAPANESE PAGODA TREE (*SOPHORA JAPONICA*)

Enjyu is a traditional Japanese dye made from the flower buds of the Japanese pagoda tree that produces a rich yellow color. The flowers, berries, and leaves of the tree are all used medicinally. The buds may be used for multiple extractions, yielding lighter dyebaths on subsequent use.

Left to right: white linen (GT & AA), silk (AT), mixed linen (GT & AA), cotton (GT & AA), linen gauze (GT & AA), white linen (GT & AA), white linen (GT & AA).
Flower buds: medium 15%, dark 25% WOF.

S

HIMALAYAN RHUBARB (*RHEUM EMODI*)

Himalayan rhubarb extract comes from the roots of the mountain rhubarb plant that grows in altitudes from 10,000–16,000ft (3,000–5,000m). It's a traditional natural dye from the Himalayan mountains. Rhubarb loves cellulose fibers. It gives deep golden tones on its own, brighter yellows when combined with aluminum salts, and shifting the pH yields almost brick reds. It also makes a great base color for overdyeing.

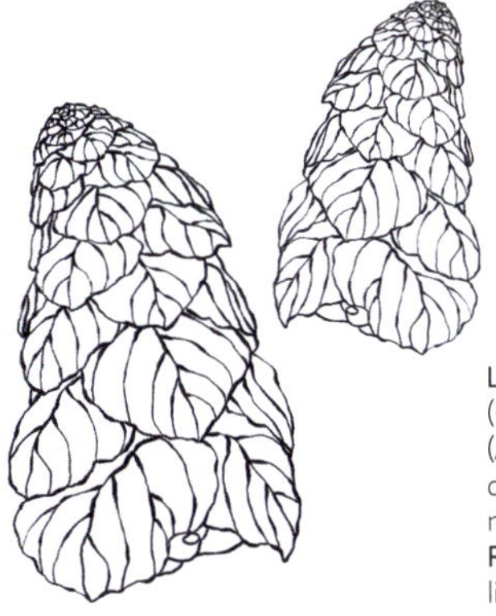

Left to right: linen gauze (GT & AA), white linen, silk (AT), white linen (GT & AA), cotton, cotton (GT & AA), mixed linen (GT & AA).
Root: 100% WOF. **Extract**: light 1–2%, medium 5–10%, dark 20% WOF.

S

PACIFIC MADRONE (*ARBUTUS MENZIESII*)

The Pacific madrone (also known as the strawberry tree) is a broadleaf evergreen tree with smooth, rich orange-red bark that peels away from the trunk and branches around the summer solstice, leaving a greenish appearance that has a satin sheen and smoothness. The tree is found on the west coast of North America, from British Columbia to California. The bark makes soft, earthy peaches, while the leaves make beautiful yellows.

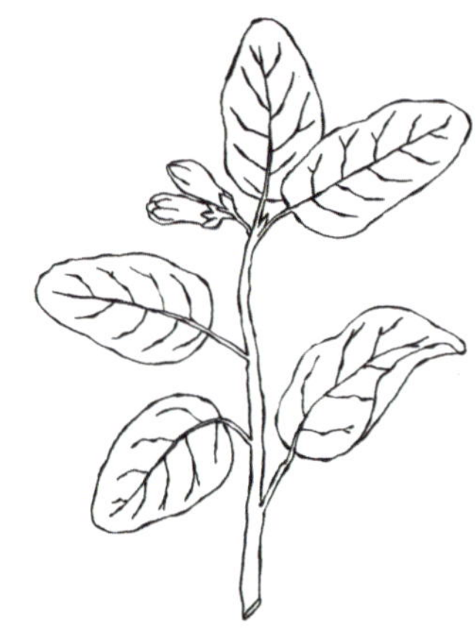

Left to right: silk, white linen, linen gauze (GT & AA), wool, cotton (GT & AA), mixed linen (GT & AA), silk (GT & AA). **Bark**: 50–100% WOF.

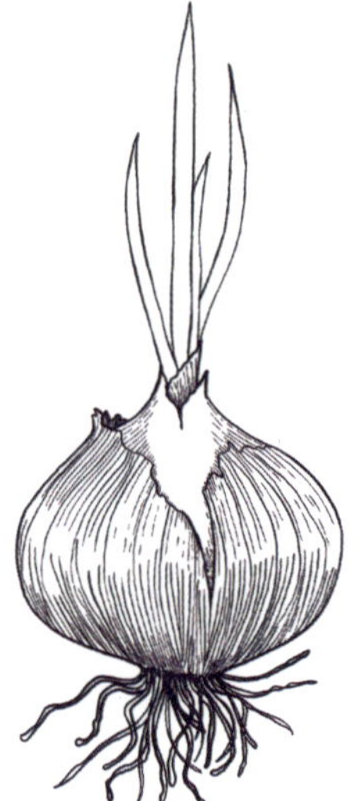

S

YELLOW ONION (*ALLIUM CEPA*)

Onion skins are a beautiful, easy, and inexpensive dye. I collect them when I cook and get them free at my local market. They can also be purchased online. Onion skins make a very pungent dyebath that yields colors ranging from warm gold to rich orange and rust. Modifying with iron will create green tones. Mordanting with aluminum salts increases lightfastness.

Left to right: linen gauze, white linen (GT & AA), silk (AT), white linen, cotton, silk, mixed linen (GT & AA). **Dried skins**: 20–30% WOF.

S

TANNER'S SUMAC (*RHUS CORIARIA*)

Sumac is a tree native to southern Europe and western Asia. The tannin is derived mainly from the bark and traditionally used for pretreating cottons and tanning leather. There are a number of North American native sumacs including smooth sumac (*Rhus glabra*) and staghorn sumac (*Rhus typhina*) that have tannin-rich leaves, bark, and roots. Tanner's sumac imparts a light yellow on cotton and when combined with iron, creates dark shades of gray and almost black.

Top to bottom: silk, linen gauze (GT & AA), silk (AT), linen (GT & AA), linen, mixed linen (GT & AA), cotton (GT & AA). **Bark**: 100% WOF.

S

LOQUAT LEAVES (BIWANOHA) (*ERIOBOTRYA JAPONICA*)

Loquat is a hardy, subtropical tree native to southeast China. It was introduced to Japan over one thousand years ago, and the leaves make a traditional Japanese dye. What makes this natural dye unique is the variety of soft pinks, peaches, corals, and oranges that you can create depending on how the plant is processed and what mordant or modifiers are used. Longer soaking times with occasional heating can dramatically deepen the color. Fresh or dried leaves can be used.

Dry leaves, left to right: white linen, white linen (GT & AA).
Dry leaves: 100% WOF.

Fresh leaves, top to bottom: white linen (GT & AA), white linen, white linen (GT & AA), silk (AT), cotton (GT & AA), cotton, linen gauze (GT & AA).
Fresh leaves: 100–200% WOF.

S

OSAGE ORANGE (*MACLURA POMIFERA*)

Osage orange is native to Arkansas, Oklahoma, and Texas, but is now planted throughout the United States. In the 1920s and 1930s during the great Dust Bowl, it was used as a tree row windbreak to prevent soil erosion. Nowadays this beautiful and durable wood is used by bow makers and woodworkers. The sawdust milled from downed trees is used as a source of natural dye. It produces very lightfast bright yellows with an aluminum salt mordant, and lovely moss greens when iron is added to the dyebath.

Top to bottom: mixed linen (GT & AA), white linen (GT & AA), silk (AT), white linen (GT & AA), cotton (GT & AA), white linen (GT & AA), linen gauze (GT & AA).
Sawdust: medium 50%, dark 75% WOF.

A

SOURGRASS (*OXALIS PES-CAPRAE*)

Sourgrass, also known as Bermuda buttercup, is one of the wildflowers that cover California in a blanket of yellow during late winter and spring. Sourgrass grows everywhere, including roadsides, lawns, and vacant lots. The flowers are the main source of color. Depending on the modifier and pH of the dyebath, colors can range from fluorescent yellows to ochers, dark greens, rusty oranges, and deep browns.

Top to bottom: white linen (GT & AA), linen gauze (GT & AA), white linen (GT & AA), mixed linen (GT & AA), silk (AT). **Fresh flowers**: 200% WOF.

A

SULFUR COSMOS (*COSMOS SULPHUREUS*)

There are so many reasons to explore sulfur cosmos. Dried or fresh flowers produce brilliant oranges to soft yellows and pale tangerines on cellulose or protein fibers. An iron afterbath shifts colors to greens and rich browns. If you grow these flowers in your garden, they will attract bees, hummingbirds, and butterflies, depending on where you live.

Left to right: silk (AT), mixed linen (GT & AA), linen gauze (GT & AA), white linen (GT & AA), white linen (GT & AA), white linen (GT & AA).
Dried flowers: 100% WOF.

A

CALENDULA (*CALENDULA OFFICINALIS*)

Calendula (pot marigold) is a popular, drought-tolerant garden plant. It is one of the easiest herbs to grow and a highly versatile medicinal plant. Its golden orange flowers are like sunshine incarnate, and the dye color is like dappled sunlight.

Left to right: linen gauze (GT & AA), silk (GT & AA), white linen (GT & AA), mixed linen (GT & AA), white linen (GT & AA).
Fresh flowers: 100% WOF.

Dried, left to right: white linen (GT & AA), white linen (GT & AA), silk (AT), mixed linen (GT & AA), linen gauze.
Dried: 100% WOF.

Fresh, left to right: cotton (GT & AA), silk (GT & AA), linen gauze (GT & AA), white linen (GT & AA), white linen (GT & AA).
Fresh: 100–200% WOF.

A

PERICÓN (*TAGETES LUCIDA*)

Pericón is a plant native to Mexico and Central America, used medicinally, in cooking, and as a dye. It has many names, including Mexican tarragon, Mexican mint, and Mexican marigold. Its color yield is light to deep gold, and the plant smells beautifully of anise. Pericón is part of the traditional dye plant palette of the Zapotec people in Oaxaca, Mexico. It can be grown in a home garden or purchased dried.

A

YAMAMOMO (*MYRICA RUBRA*)

Yamamomo (Chinese bayberry) is a subtropical, broadleaf evergreen fruit tree used for making jam, fruit wine, and vinegar. It is also used in traditional medicine. The branches are chipped to make this traditional Japanese dye, which has been used since the Nara period (710–794 CE) and was popular as an overdye during the Edo period (1603–1868). Colors range from warm yellow-green to slightly bronze-yellow. Yamamomo chips may be used for multiple extractions to yield lighter dyebaths.

Top to bottom: mixed linen (GT & AA), white linen (GT & AA), cotton (GT & AA), silk (AT), linen gauze (GT & AA), white linen (GT & AA). **Bark**: 50% WOF.

A

WELD (*RESEDA LUTEOLA*)

Weld—or dyer's rocket, as it is also known—is the strongest, most lightfast source for natural yellow dye. It's the brightest and clearest yellow flower dye. In combination with iron, weld creates vivid chartreuse. Weld can be purchased as dried flowers or an extract. It's also perfect for planting in the dye garden. The flowers are beautifully fragrant and great for luring in pollinators. Both fresh and dried weld produce strong color.

Left to right: linen gauze (GT & AA), silk (AT), white linen (GT & AA), cotton (GT & AA), cotton (GT & AA), white linen (GT & AA), mixed linen (GT & AA). **Dried plant:** 100% WOF. **Extract:** light 0.25–1%, medium 2–3%, dark 4–6% WOF.

S

WILD CHERRY (*PRUNUS AVIUM*)

Wild cherry and fruitwood chips from cultivated cherry, peach, apricot, and plum trees can be used to make a variety of beautiful soft peaches and peachy pinks. I love using wild cherry bark. The longer the bark is allowed to soak, the more pigment is extracted. The colors begin as soft peaches and, after a couple of days, they shift to soft oranges and terracotta.

Left to right: linen gauze, linen gauze, silk, wool, linen gauze (GT & AA), white linen (GT & AA). **Inner bark:** 100% WOF.

A

WILD FENNEL (*FOENICULUM VULGARE*)

Wild fennel (wild anise) is a non-native plant that is considered invasive in California, especially along the coast. July through August, its small, bright yellow flowers light up the roadsides, making it easy to find. The stalks, fronds, and flowers produce beautiful yellows. It hosts the larvae of the anise swallowtail butterfly, so even though it's invasive, I always leave some flowers behind when harvesting the plant for dyeing.

Top to bottom: wool (AT), white linen (GT & AA), silk (AT), mixed linen (GT & AA), linen gauze (GT & AA), cotton (GT & AA), white linen (GT & AA).
Flowers and foliage combined: 200% WOF.

Greens and Turquoise

A

BLACK HOLLYHOCK (*ALCEA ROSEA NIGRA*)

Black hollyhocks are a uniquely colored variety that has been a favorite of gardeners and botanists for nearly four hundred years. When used as a natural dye, this gothic flower creates dramatic purples, teals, periwinkle blue, and slate grays depending on your water pH and choice of mordant. All you need is a handful of fresh or dried blooms.

Top to bottom: mixed linen (GT & AA), wool (AT), silk (AT), linen gauze (GT & AA), white linen (GT & AA), white linen (GT & AA), white linen (GT & AA).
Dried flowers: 100% WOF.

Leaves, left to right: linen gauze (GT & AA), cotton, linen, silk (AT), wool, linen (GT & AA), mixed linen (GT & AA).
Leaves: 100–300% WOF.

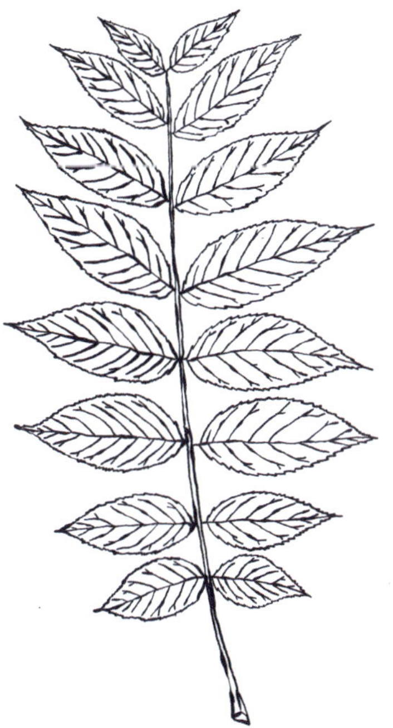

S

SOUTHERN CALIFORNIA BLACK WALNUT (*JUGLANS CALIFORNICA*)

Black walnut is native to the United States and widely planted in temperate areas throughout the world. The tannin-rich leaves create a pungent and pigment-rich dyebath. The husks, catkins, bark, and heartwood can also be used. Using different mordants increases the range of colors you can create. Gloves should be worn when handling leaves and husks to avoiding staining the skin. A combination of logwood, walnut husks, and iron creates rich, earthy, almost-black colors.

Nut husks, left to right: linen (GT & AA), linen, silk, silk (AT).
Nut husks: 100–200% WOF.

A

BRACKEN FERN (*PTERIDIUM AQUILINUM*)

Bracken is a very aggressive fern found worldwide in oak and pine forests, on hillsides or open pastures, and by dry woodlands. It has broad, triangular fronds and reaches heights of 2–4ft (60–120cm). Depending on the time of year, bracken yields soft yellows, olives, and browns with green undertones. Bracken has deep roots in folklore and is thought to bestow luck, good health, and riches when carried.

Left to right: silk (AT), wool (GT & AA), white linen (GT & AA), cotton (GT & AA), white linen (GT & AA), white linen (GT & AA).
Foliage: 100% WOF.

A

WHITE MULBERRY (*MORUS ALBA*)

Chlorophyll, in its raw state, is not a stable natural dye. Chlorophyllin is extracted from mulberry leaves and is treated with metal salts to make it water-soluble and stable. The resulting dark green powder smells of green tea and yields soft, clear seafoam to emerald greens. It's not a robust dye, but it adds a nice pop of green to any color story.

Left to right: linen gauze (GT & AA), mixed linen (GT & AA), white linen (GT & AA), silk (AT), white linen (GT & AA), cotton (GT & AA).
Extract: light 1–2%, medium 3–4%, dark 5–10% WOF.

A

YARROW (*ACHILLEA MILLEFOLIUM*)

YELLOW YARROW (*ERIOPHYLLUM CONFERTIFLORUM*)

Yarrow is native to Asia, Europe, and North America. It's found in grasslands, fields, and open forests with mildly disturbed soil. The flowers begin to bloom in early summer through fall, depending on the climate. The color of the flower will impact the natural dye color: white and yellow are the most common, but colors can range from soft pink and coral to orange and red. It's high in tannin, but stronger colors only reveal themselves on cellulose fibers when mordanted with aluminum salts.

Common yarrow, left to right: white linen (GT & AA), wool, silk (AT), cotton (GT & AA), linen gauze, mixed linen (GT & AA), white linen (GT & AA).
Flowers and foliage combined: 100% WOF.

Yellow yarrow, left to right: linen, wool (AT), mixed linen (GT & AA), linen (GT & AA), linen gauze (GT & AA), silk (AT), cotton (GT & AA).
Flowers and foliage combined: 100% WOF.

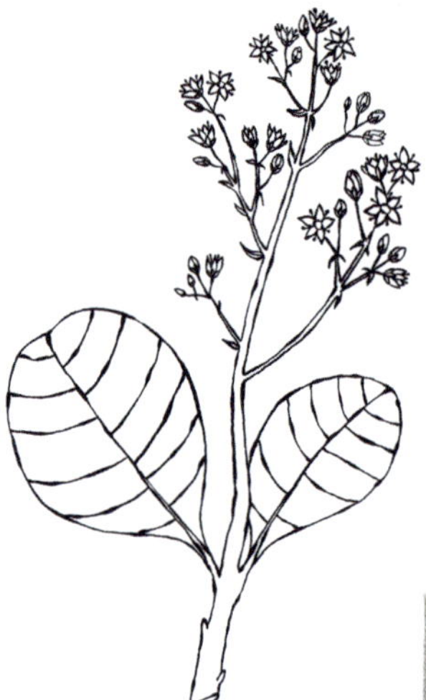

A

SMOKE BUSH (*COTINUS COGGYGRIA*)

The smoke bush (smoketree) has deep purple-red foliage and gets its name from the wispy clumps of pink flowers that look like puffs of smoke. Use the pruned branches and leaves to create dusty, peacock blues. Dyeables should be handwashed to maintain the color; if machine-washed, the colors shift to lovely grays. It's best for dyeing ribbon or other decorative embellishments. Purple-leaved plum tree (*Prunus cerasifera nigra*) is a good substitution.

Left to right: mixed linen (GT & AA), linen (GT & AA), cotton (GT & AA), linen gauze (GT & AA), linen (GT & AA, modified with white vinegar), linen (GT & AA, modified with soda ash), silk (GT & AA).
Leaves: 100–200% WOF.

A

MUGWORT (*ARTEMISIA VULGARIS*)

Mugwort is named after the Greek goddess Artemis. This fragrant herb has been celebrated across various cultures for its medicinal benefits and is one of the first plants to appear in the springtime along roadsides, in open meadows, and even urban environments. It yields beautiful silvery greens with fresh leaves and can also be used dry with subtle variations to the color. I used California mugwort (*Artemisia douglasiana*) to dye these swatches.

Left to right: silk (AT), cotton (GT & AA), white linen (GT & AA), white linen (GT & AA), linen gauze (GT & AA), mixed linen (GT & AA).
Foliage: 100–200% WOF.

S

SILK TREE (*ALBIZIA JULIBRISSIN*)

Silk tree (Persian silk tree) is native to southwestern and eastern Asia and was introduced to the United States in the eighteenth century. The flowers and bark of this tree are used in traditional Chinese medicine. Silk trees bloom from May through July and are easy to spot due to their almost fern-like leaves and silky, pink, pom-pom-esque flowers. Use an aluminum salt mordant for strong vibrant chartreuse colors on cellulose fibers.

Top to bottom: white linen (GT & AA), silk, cotton, cotton (GT & AA), mixed linen (GT & AA), white linen (GT & AA). **Leaves:** 100–200% WOF.

August harvest, left to right: mixed linen (GT & AA), linen gauze (GT & AA), white linen (GT & AA), silk (AT), wool (AT), cotton (GT & AA), white linen (GT & AA).
Foliage: 100–200% WOF.

A

STINGING NETTLE (*URTICA DIOICA*)

Nettle is found in forests, gardens, and ditches. Originally native to Europe, parts of Asia, and North Africa, it's now found worldwide. Nettle is edible, medicinal, and makes beautiful cordage and cloth. As a natural dye, it creates colors ranging from yellow to khaki and olive greens, depending on the time of year.

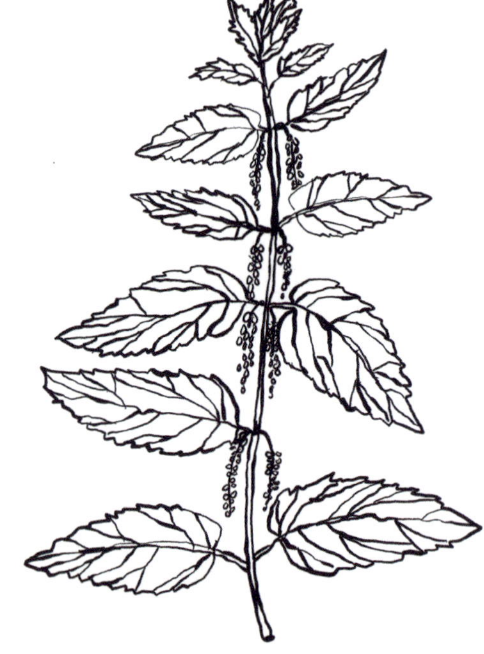

May harvest, left to right: mixed linen (GT & AA), linen gauze (GT & AA), white linen (GT & AA), silk (AT), wool (AT), cotton (GT & AA), white linen (GT & AA).
Foliage: 100–200% WOF.

Top to bottom: white wool (AT), silk (AT), mixed linen (GT & AA), white linen (GT & AA), white cotton (GT & AA), white linen gauze (GT & AA), white linen (GT & AA). **Foliage**: 100–200% WOF.

A

ST. JOHN'S WORT (*HYPERICUM PERFORATUM*)

St. John's wort is one of my favorite plants. It blooms around the summer solstice and can be found in most places throughout the world. If you pinch the bright yellow flowers between your fingers, they leave a purplish red mark. I generally use the stems and leaves for dyeing and save the flowers for medicine, but I always include a few in the dyebath. Colors range from vibrant greens to olives and, as the dyebath ages and becomes exhausted, the colors shift to golden yellows.

Browns, Grays, Tans, and Creams

Leaves, left to right: linen gauze, white linen (GT & AA), white linen, cotton (GT & AA), white linen (GT & AA), cotton, silk (AT).
Leaves: 100–200% WOF.

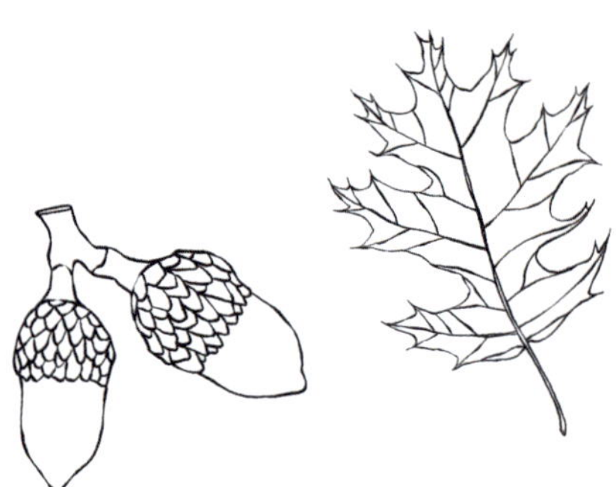

S

CALIFORNIA BLACK OAK (*QUERCUS KELLOGGII*)

There is nothing quite as majestic as the black oak tree, especially at the ripe old age of six hundred years. Black oaks, white oaks, live oaks, and other species all yield different colors. All parts of the tree are high in tannin, and the leaves and acorns produce beautiful, quiet colors ranging from ivories to blushing tans. Aluminum salt mordants shift colors toward gold, and iron creates a wide range of grays.

Acorns, left to right: linen (GT & AA), linen, silk (AT), linen gauze (GT & AA), cotton (GT & AA).
Acorns: 100–200% WOF.

Root, left to right: white linen, silk, linen gauze, wool, mixed linen, white linen.
Root: 100–300% WOF.

Seeds and leaves, left to right: linen gauze (GT & AA), cotton (GT & AA), silk (AT), white linen (GT & AA), mixed linen (GT & AA), white linen (GT & AA), white linen (GT & AA), white linen (GT & AA, using leaves only).
Seeds and leaves: 100–200% WOF.

S

CURLY DOCK ROOT (*RUMEX CRISPUS*)

Curly dock (also, yellow dock) has its origins in Europe and made its way to North America with early settlers. Various parts of the plant are edible and the roots are used in herbal medicine. The roots are a substantive dye, and the leaves and seeds produce a variety of colors depending on the mordant used. You can create an entire color story with different parts of this plant.

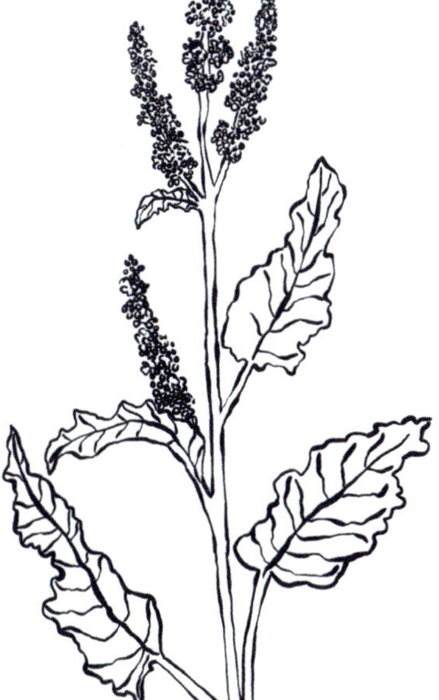

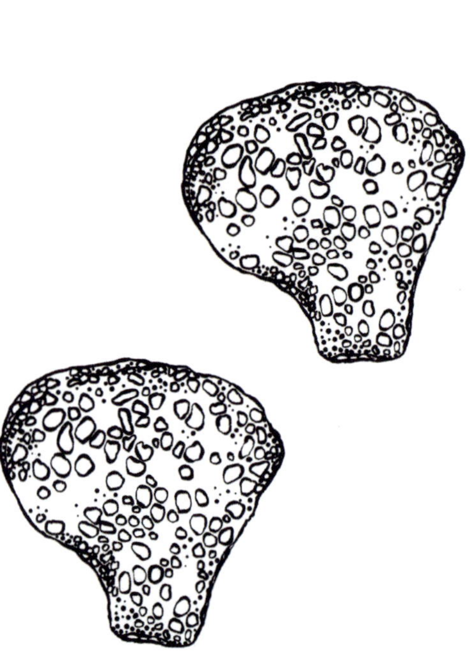

S

DYEBALL MUSHROOM (*PISOLITHUS ARRHIZUS*)

Also known as dead man's foot, the dyeball mushroom is found throughout North America and across southern Europe. Look for this fungus in late summer and early fall. It grows in open, disturbed areas with sandy soil, along hiking trails, runoff ditches, and areas with poor soil quality. It's best to harvest the mushroom when it's young and filled with spore packets and a blackish ooze. Once the spores dry, they're much harder to dissolve in water. The addition of glycerin or dish soap helps the dried spores dissolve.

Top to bottom: silk, white linen, white linen (GT & AA), wool, cotton (GT & AA), linen gauze (GT & AA), silk (GT & AA).
Mushroom: 100% WOF.

S

BEAKED HAZEL (*CORYLUS CORNUTA*)

The hazel tree is native to the United States, Europe, and western Asia. Hazel hedges provide windbreaks, visual screens, and food and shelter for wildlife. The leaves and soft twigs produce lovely shades of ivory without a mordant, and golden tans with an aluminum salt mordant.

Left to right: mixed linen (GT & AA), white linen (GT & AA), linen gauze, silk, white linen, cotton (GT & AA), cotton. **Leaves:** 200–400% WOF.

A

HOLLY (*ILEX AQUIFOLIUM*)

Holly is an evergreen tree with leathery leaves and red berries. In folklore, holly was traditionally planted near houses to offer protection from lightning. We now know the spines on the leaves can act as miniature lightning conductors that protect the tree and other objects nearby. Holly leaves create soft, silvery greens on cellulose and silk fabric, but can also create browns depending on the season.

Left to right: white wool (GT & AA), silk (AT), mixed linen, white linen (GT & AA), white linen, linen gauze, white wool. **Leaves:** 100–300% WOF.

Nut husks, left to right: silk, wool, white linen, silk (AT), white linen (GT & AA), linen gauze.
Nut husks: 100–200% WOF.

S

ENGLISH WALNUT (*JUGLANS REGIA*)

English walnut trees have origins in Iran, but have been cultivated in central Asia and China for two thousand years, and throughout Europe from Roman times or earlier. They were introduced to the Americas in the seventeenth century by English colonists. Like the black walnut (see page 115), all parts of the tree are substantive and produce colors. Using different mordants increases the range of colors on fabric. The colors yielded are soft browns with yellow undertones.

Leaves, left to right: linen gauze (GT & AA), mixed linen (GT & AA), linen gauze, silk (AT), wool (AT), white linen, white linen (GT & AA).
Leaves: 200–300% WOF.

A

SHEEP SORREL (*RUMEX ACETOSELLA*)

Sheep sorrel (also known as field sorrel) is a perennial herb in the buckwheat family. Its young, tender leaves are edible. The plant is self-seeding with a quickly spreading root system; it is a very invasive weed and is banned from planting in some areas. Look for sheep sorrel in sunny, open, disturbed areas, such as pastures, meadows, ditches, and roadsides. Harvest stalks and seeds in late summer and through the fall after they turn reddish brown. The colors produced can range from earthy pinks to tans depending on growing conditions and harvest times.

Top to bottom: linen gauze (GT & AA), linen (GT & AA), silk (GT & AA), cotton (GT & AA).
Foliage: 200–300% WOF.

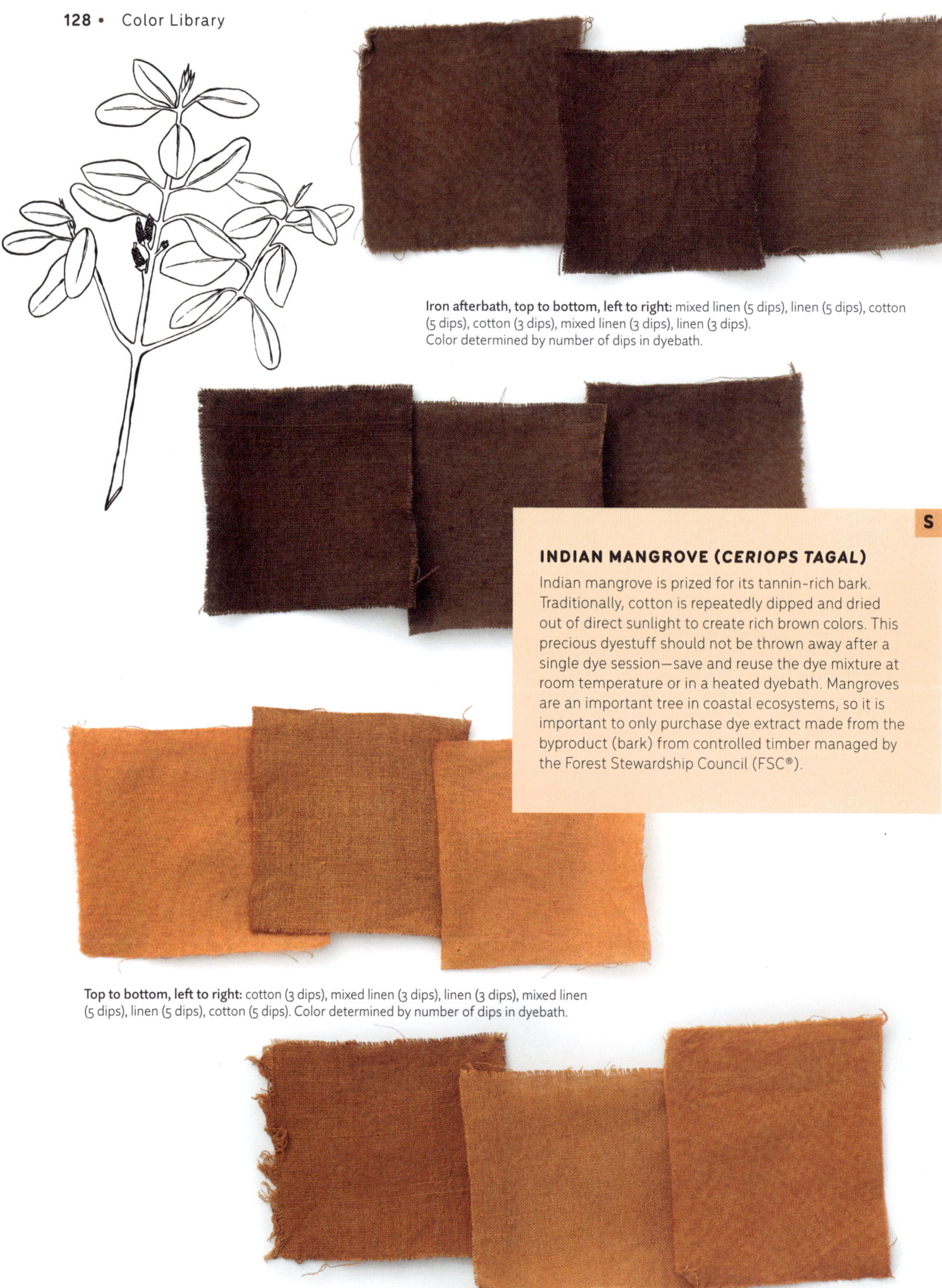

Iron afterbath, top to bottom, left to right: mixed linen (5 dips), linen (5 dips), cotton (5 dips), cotton (3 dips), mixed linen (3 dips), linen (3 dips).
Color determined by number of dips in dyebath.

S

INDIAN MANGROVE (*CERIOPS TAGAL*)

Indian mangrove is prized for its tannin-rich bark. Traditionally, cotton is repeatedly dipped and dried out of direct sunlight to create rich brown colors. This precious dyestuff should not be thrown away after a single dye session—save and reuse the dye mixture at room temperature or in a heated dyebath. Mangroves are an important tree in coastal ecosystems, so it is important to only purchase dye extract made from the byproduct (bark) from controlled timber managed by the Forest Stewardship Council (FSC®).

Top to bottom, left to right: cotton (3 dips), mixed linen (3 dips), linen (3 dips), mixed linen (5 dips), linen (5 dips), cotton (5 dips). Color determined by number of dips in dyebath.

A

JUNIPER (*JUNIPERUS COMMUNIS*)

Juniper takes a variety of forms, from tall evergreen trees to shrubs, and is best known for flavoring gin. Its needle-like leaves and berries have a pleasant smell and can be used separately or combined to create a dyebath. They yield colors ranging from champagne and light yellow ochers to khaki and soft peachy tans, depending on the time of year.

Left to right: linen gauze (GT & AA), silk, cotton, cotton (GT & AA), mixed linen (GT & AA), white linen (GT & AA), white linen (GT & AA).
Foliage: 100–200% WOF.

S

JAPANESE PERSIMMON (*DIOSPYROS KAKI*)

Kakishibu is a tannin-rich solution made from unripened persimmons that have been fermented and aged for more than two years. It's an important color in the Japanese palette. The color is developed by repeatedly soaking fabric and exposing it to sunlight. The true magic of Kakishibu is revealed over time, as the color becomes deeper through the oxidation of the tannin and continued exposure to sunlight.

Iron afterbath, top to bottom, left to right: linen gauze (1 dip), cotton (1 dip), linen (1 dip), linen gauze (3 dips), linen (3 dips), cotton (3 dips), cotton (5 dips), linen (5 dips), linen gauze (5 dips).
Color determined by number of dips in dyebath.

Top to bottom, left to right: cotton (1 dip), linen (1 dip), linen gauze (1 dip), cotton (3 dips), linen (3 dips), linen gauze (3 dips), cotton (5 dips), linen (5 dips), linen gauze (5 dips).
Color determined by number of dips in dyebath.

S

TANOAK (*NOTHOLITHOCARPUS DENSIFLORUS*)

Tanoak (or tanbark-oak) is a false oak, the bark of which is used in the tanning industry. It is native to the far western United States, found in California and Oregon. The leaves are rich in tannins and produce lovely shades of soft peachy pinks with tan undertones, depending on the time of year.

Top to bottom: silk, cotton (GT & AA), linen gauze, linen gauze (GT & AA), mixed linen (GT & AA), white linen (GT & AA), white linen.
Leaves: 100–200% WOF.

S

BLACK MYROBALAN (*TERMINALIA CHEBULA*)

Myrobalan dye comes from the ground nuts of the myrobalan tree, which grows throughout India, primarily in the foothills of the Himalayas. It's high in tannins and may be used either alone as a dye, or in combination with aluminum salts and iron. It makes buttery yellow and tan, and is a good foundation color for overdyeing. With the addition of iron, use a higher percentage to create brown and black on cellulose fabrics.

Left to right: linen (GT & AA), cotton, cotton (GT & AA), linen gauze (GT & AA), silk (AT), linen, mixed linen (GT & AA).
Extract: light 2–3%, medium 5–8%, dark 10–13% WOF.

S

OAK APPLE WASP GALLS (*TRICHOTERAS VACCINIFOLIAE*)

Oak galls are spheres that grow on white oaks and come in many shapes and sizes. They first appear glossy and green in the spring, and are home to gall wasps. Harvest in August through October once they've turned creamy tan, with small holes visible on the surface, ensuring the wasps have hatched. Gather them before the rainy season for the highest tannin content. Oak apple galls yield a variety of champagne colors. For beautiful cool grays, use a pinch of iron.

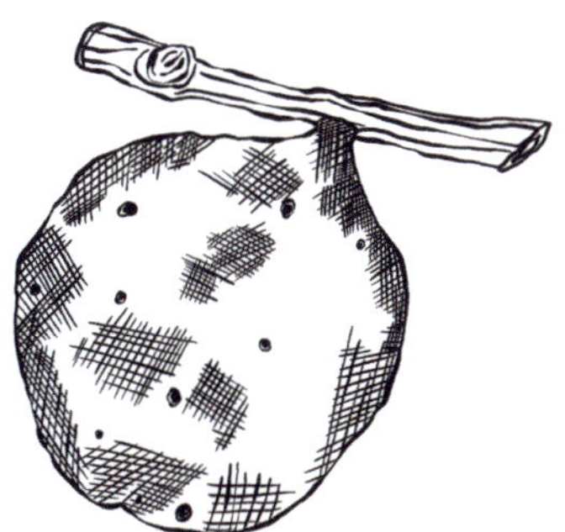

Left to right: white linen (GT & AA), linen gauze, silk, cotton, mixed linen (GT & AA), white linen, wool.
Dried: 50–100% WOF.

S

SOUTHERN BLUE GUM (*EUCALYPTUS GLOBULUS*)

Blue gum is one of many species of eucalyptus native to Australia. It was introduced into California for wood, shelter, landscaping, and for its curative powers. The bark sheds in long strips and is easy to gather in late summer through to fall. Both the bark and leaves are used for natural dye. Only use this dye outside; it's highly aromatic and some people have adverse reactions to it. Blue gum leaves yield a green color, while orange and peach tones can be obtained from the bark. To yield a stronger color, pour boiling water over the bark and allow it to soak for several days to a week before boiling it again.

Bark, left to right: linen gauze (GT & AA), linen, linen (GT & AA), cotton, cotton (GT & AA), silk, silk (AT).
Bark: 100–200% WOF.

Leaves, left to right: linen, linen (GT & AA), cotton, linen (GT & AA), silk, linen gauze (GT & AA), mixed linen (GT & AA).
Leaves: 100–200% WOF.

S

SWEET CHESTNUT (*CASTANEA SATIVA*)

The sweet chestnut tree has been used historically for tanning leather in Europe and North America. It's a rich source of tannin and can be used as a natural dye or a mordant. Chestnut yields a soft yellow, which is excellent for combining with other natural dyes to add subtle nuances to your color palette. Chestnut is well known for its ability to dye silk black with the addition of logwood and iron.

Top to bottom: cotton (GT & AA), cotton, mixed linen (GT & AA), linen, linen (GT & AA), linen gauze (GT & AA), silk.
Extract: light 1–3%, medium 5–8%, dark 10% WOF.

S

TEA (*CAMELLIA SINENSIS*)

Tea is the most popular beverage in the world besides water, and one of the most overlooked and underrated natural dyes. It's rich in tannins and works beautifully on both protein and cellulose fibers. There are myriad quiet colors you can obtain from black and green teas. Black tea can also be used as an overdye to antique or subdue colors. Combining tea with mineral salts will expand the range of color even further.

Green tea, left to right: white linen, white linen (GT & AA), linen gauze (GT & AA).
Dried tea leaves: 100% WOF.

Black tea, left to right: white linen, white linen (GT & AA), linen gauze (GT & AA).
Dried tea leaves: 50–100% WOF.

Pu-erh tea, left to right: white linen, white linen (GT & AA), linen gauze (GT & AA).
Dried tea leaves: 50–100% WOF.

S

TARA (*CAESALPINIA TINCTORIA*)

Tara is the Quecha name for the shrubby tree *Caesalpinia tinctoria*; it is also known as Peruvian carob. Native to South America, the seed pods of the tree have traditional medicinal uses and are also the source of the dye. Tara powder is high in gallic acid, making it ideal for mordanting and tanning leather. It has a tea-like aroma and imparts no color on fabric but makes beautiful purple-grays when you add a pinch of iron to the dyebath.

Iron afterbath, left to right: silk (AT), silk, linen, linen (GT & AA), cotton (GT & AA), linen gauze (GT & AA), mixed linen (GT & AA). **Extract**: 10% WOF. **Iron**: 1–2% WOF.

A

ARROYO WILLOW (*SALIX LASIOLEPSIS*)

Willow is part of a large family of deciduous trees and shrubs with an affinity for water. It blooms early at a critical time in the life cycle of many native bees, and is an important host plant to moths and butterflies. Willow leaves yield silvery greens, grays, and yellows depending on the species and the time of year the leaves are gathered. Use the older leaves that get a lot of direct sunlight for a stronger color.

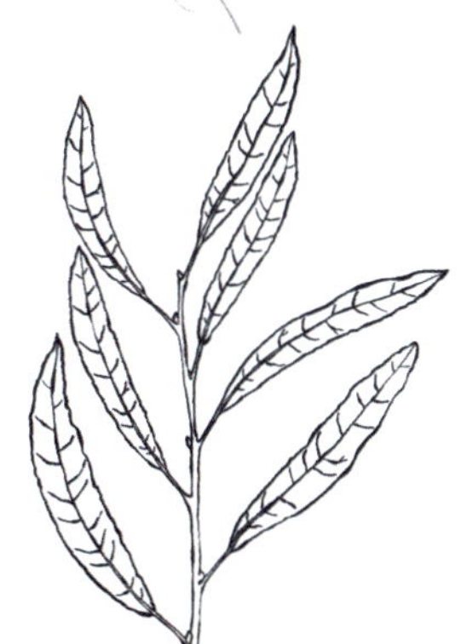

Left to right: linen gauze (GT & AA), linen gauze, cotton, linen, silk (AT), wool (AT), mixed linen (GT & AA). **Leaves**: 200–400% WOF.

Glossary

Adjective dyes do not bond to the fiber on their own and require a mordant. A tannin, mineral salt mordant, or a combination of both, must be applied before the fiber is dyed. A few examples of adjective dyes are cochineal, marigold, other flowers, and nettles.

Afterbath refers to a secondary bath containing a modifier that a dyed textile is submerged in for a set amount of time, resulting in a shift in color.

Dyebath is a solution of water and plant-derived pigment that is used to dye natural fibers.

Exhaust bath is a dyebath that has already been used for dyeing and has very little dye remaining.

Lightfast is a dye's ability to resist fading when exposed to UV light.

Modifiers are solutions used to change the color of the dyed fabric or fiber, to broaden the spectrum. Modifiers can be acidic, alkaline, or metallic salt.

Mordant is a mineral salt that helps natural dyes adhere to fibers and textiles such as wool, cotton, or silk. A mordant solution ensures more colorfast, washfast, and lightfast results. It also affects the color outcomes of the dye.

Nonreactive refers to a material that doesn't react chemically with an acidic substance. Stainless steel, ceramic, glass, and metal cookware with enamel coating are all nonreactive materials. Reactive materials—such as aluminum, iron, tin, and copper—can leach into solutions and cause color changes.

Overdye is to dye fabric that has already been dyed. This can be a second application of the same color, layering or refreshing the color, or a secondary color. Fabric can be overdyed with multiple colors. Generally, using more than three different colors will result in muddy or murky shades.

pH is a scale that measures how acidic or alkaline a water-based solution is: 0–6 is acidic or low pH, 7 is pH neutral, and 8–14 is alkaline, high pH, or basic. You can test the pH-level of water or a solution with litmus paper (pH strips) or a pH meter.

Stop bath is a secondary pot of hot water, similar in temperature to the dyebath. Temperature can range from 140–180°F (60–82°C) and is used to complete the dyeing process. Once the desired color is achieved, the fabric is moved to the stop bath to finish the hour-long heated bath.

Substantive dyes are often high in tannin and do not need a mordant to bond to the fiber. However, using a mordant can improve results, often expanding the range and depths of color. Some examples of substantive dyes are tree bark, walnut leaves, pomegranate husks, tea, and field horsetail.

Just to confuse things, some dyes are substantive on protein fibers but not cellulose fibers. This includes logwood, although lightfastness and washfastness are always improved with the addition of a mineral salt mordant.

Tannins are clear, yellowish or reddish brown water-soluble compounds found in some galls, tree barks, leaves, unripe fruit, nuts, and other plant tissues, consisting of gallic or tannic acid. They are used as tanning agents, mordants, ink, and in natural dyeing.

Underdye is when you apply a base color with the intention of then overdyeing to achieve a particular color. It also refers to applying a colored (ellegic or catechic) tannin. Generally, this is a light application that is done in conjunction with an aluminum salt mordant to enrich the natural dye color.

Washfast is a dye's ability to resist fading or bleeding in the presence of water.

Suppliers and Resources

Aurora Silk (aurorasilk.com/wp/)
Natural dyes, fabrics, and dyeables
International shipping, located in the US

Bloom & Dye (bloomanddye.com)
Natural dyes
International shipping, located in the US

Botanical Colors (botanicalcolors.com)
Natural dyes, fabrics, and dyeables, seeds, blog
International shipping, located in the US

Cochinillas Guatiza (cochinillasguatiza.com)
Premium handmade cochineal
International shipping, located in the Canary Islands

Dharma Trading Co. (dharmatrading.com)
Natural dyes, fabrics, and dyeables
International shipping, located in the US

Earth Guild (earthguild.com)
Natural dyes, fabrics, and dyeables
International shipping, located in the US

Fabrics-store.com (fabrics-store.com)
Linen, linen blends, and cotton fabric
International shipping, located in the US

Good Gray (goodgray.com)
Specialty stationery and art supplies
Ships to the US only

Grand Prismatic Seed (grandprismaticseed.com)
Seeds and natural dyes
Ships to the US only

Jet Pens (jetpens.com)
Specialty stationery and art supplies
International shipping, located in the US

Maiwa (maiwa.com)
Natural dyes, fabrics, and dyeables
International shipping, located in Canada

Michel Garcia (michelgarcia.fr)
Natural dyes
International shipping, located in France

Mountain Rose Herbs (mountainroseherbs.com)
Seeds and dyer's alkanet
Ships to the US, US territories, and Canada only

Soil to Soil Market (soiltosoilmarket.com)
Seeds and natural dyes
International shipping, located in the US

Themázi (themazi.com)
Natural dyes, fabrics, and dyeables, blog
International shipping, located in Turkey

Traditional Tanners (braintan.com)
Tannins and natural dyes
International shipping, located in the US

Vreseis Limited (vreseis.com)
Organic cotton
International shipping, located in the US

Wild Colours (wildcolours.co.uk)
Natural dyes
International shipping, located in the UK

Yoseka Stationery (yosekastationery.com)
Specialty stationery and art supplies
International shipping, located in the US

Books

Behan, Babs, *Botanical Inks: Plant-to-Print Dyes, Techniques and Projects* (Quadrille, 2018)

Beeler, Julie, *The Mushroom Color Atlas: A Guide to Dyes and Pigments Made from Fungi* (Chronicle Books, 2024)

Boutrup, Joy and Ellis, Catharine, *The Art and Science of Natural Dyes: Principles, Experiments, and Results* (Schiffer Craft, 2019)

Burgess, Rebecca, *Harvesting Color: How to Find Plants and Make Natural Dyes* (Artisan, 2011)

Casselman, Karen Leigh, *Craft of the Dyer: Colour from Plants and Lichens*, Dover Crafts: Weaving & Dyeing, (Dover Publications, 2nd rev. edn, 1993)

Cannon, John and Margaret, *Dye Plants and Dyeing* (Timber Press, 2003)

Dean, Jenny, *Wild Color: The Complete Guide to Making and Using Natural Dyes* (Potter Craft, rev. edn, 2010)

Duerr, Sasha, *Natural Palettes: Inspiration from Plant-Based Color* (Princeton Architectural Press, 2020)

Jacobs, Betty E. M., *Growing Herbs and Plants for Dyeing* (Graphicom, 1977)

Liles, J. N., *The Art and Craft of Natural Dyeing: Traditional Recipes for Modern Use* (University of Tennessee Press, 1990)

Marianchild, Kate, *Secrets of the Oak Woodlands: Plants and Animals Among California's Oaks* (Heyday, 2013)

Richards, Lynne and Tyrl, Ronald J., *Dyes from American Native Plants: A Practical Guide* (Timber Press, 2005)

Vejar, Kristine, *The Modern Natural Dyer: A Comprehensive Guide to Dyeing Silk, Wool, Linen, and Cotton at Home* (STC Craft, 2015)

Vejar, Kristine and Rodriguez, Adrienne, *Journeys in Natural Dyeing: Techniques for Creating Color at Home* (Abrams Books, 2020)

Useful websites

Catharine Ellis (ellistextiles.com)
Website of weaver and dyer Catharine Ellis.

Threads of Life (threadsoflife.com)
A social enterprise supporting women making indigenous textiles across Indonesia. The website includes field notes, journals, and textile highlights.

Fibershed (fibershed.org)
A nonprofit organization that develops regional fiber systems that build ecosystem and community health.

Natural Dye Workshop (naturaldyeworkshop.com)
Discussion forum about the science and practice of natural dyes.

Index

Acknowledgments

There are so many people that I am grateful to for being a part of my life and making this book and all my creative adventures possible. You are beautiful magick.

To Will, my brilliant and patient husband and co-conspirator. Thank you for always supporting and encouraging me in all my creative journeys. Thank you for helping with the photoshoot by moving dye pots and buckets. This book would not have happened without you. You make my heart explode.

To my magickal friend Whitni for years of friendship and always making me smile. You took the most beautiful pictures, capturing my process and the forest. I love you to the moon and stars, and back again.

To Laurel and Andy for helping me make my outdoor dye studio a reality. Thank you from my heart of hearts.

To Ella, Emma, and Martina. My deepest gratitude for all your patience and guidance. You transformed my words and process into a beautiful book. To Lily DG for the opportunity to write this book. Thank you to everyone at Quarto.

To Lily R for spending the day helping me label hundreds of naturally dyed fabric samples. There is no way I would have been able to do it without you.

To Bradley, thank you for helping me understand the process of writing a book, editing my bio, and drinking champagne with me.

To Kathy Hatori and Amy DuFault for inviting me to share my process on Feed Back Friday. You created a beautiful, safe space and an incredible creative community during "Shelter in Place" and beyond. I will always be so thankful for you both.

To Rebecca Burgess, thank you for introducing me to natural dyes and the beautiful Fibershed community.

To my Grandma Bernice for teaching me the love of making things. I dedicate this book to your memory.

To all the natural dyers for sharing their processes and experiments.

To my beautiful creative community, thank you for all your sweet words and encouragement. Thank you to everyone who has taken workshops and purchased naturally dyed thread, fabric, and patchwork patterns from me. A special thanks to everyone who supports me on Patreon, I'm so lucky to have you. Without all of you, this book would not have been possible.

To my beautiful forest and all the surrounding landscape for sharing your hidden colors with me.